HAUNTED
INNS OF
BRITAIN & IRELAND

HAUNTED
INNS OF
BRITAIN & IRELAND

RICHARD JONES

NEW
HOLLAND

First published in 2004 by
New Holland Publishers (UK) Ltd
London • Cape Town • Sydney • Auckland

www.newhollandpublishers.com

Garfield House
86–88 Edgware Road
London W2 2EA
United Kingdom

80 McKenzie Street
Cape Town 8001
South Africa

14 Aquatic Drive
Frenchs Forest, NSW 2086
Australia

218 Lake Road
Northcote
Auckland
New Zealand

ISBN 1 84330 732 4

Publishing Manager: Jo Hemmings
Editor: Deborah Taylor
Designer: Gülen Shevki
Production: Joan Woodroffe
Cartographer: Bill Smuts
Illustrator: Phil Garner

Front cover: The Red Lion Inn, Avebury (page 30)
Spine: The Choughs Hotel, Chard (page 22)
Back cover: The Whittington Inn, Kinver (page 107)

Reproduction by Pica Digital (Pte) Ltd, Singapore
Printed and bound by Kyodo Printing Co (Singapore) Ltd

CONTENTS

INTRODUCTION

In September 2002 I undertook the first leg of a journey that would, over the next eight months, take me to some wonderfully atmospheric old inns dotted across the spectral landscape of Britain and Ireland. With somewhere in the region of 60,000 inns to choose from, the first hurdle was to work out which ones were haunted and, of those, which were worth including. I was able to fall back on the stories collected by those inexhaustible researchers who had gone before me – and I must acknowledge a huge debt of gratitude to Marc Alexander, Andrew Green, Jack Hallam and Peter Underwood in this respect – but I soon discovered that previous books on the subject had been, on the whole, unrepresentative of Scotland, Wales and, in particular, of Ireland. I wanted to include several inns whose ghost stories had never been published, so I began by sending a generic e-mail to almost 900 potential hostelries asking if they were haunted and, if so, whether there would be any objection to my using their stories.

Having whittled the list down to around 250, I set off on my journey. I had not been particularly successful in finding haunted inns in either Ireland or Wales, so in both these countries I resorted to simply stopping at likely looking inns and asking the bar staff or owners if the place was haunted. I quickly discovered that there was a natural reluctance on the part of some managers to admit that their premises had a ghost, for fear of deterring potential guests. Consequently (in addition to the much-cracked quip, 'The only spirits here are behind the bar'), quite a few of the ghost stories I collected tended to be somewhat vague: glasses 'mysteriously' falling off shelves, for example, or staff experiencing the unnerving feeling that they were being watched by an invisible 'someone' or 'something' as they went about their duties.

The main problem I encountered was that, in the past 15 or so years, the pub scene in Britain and Ireland has witnessed dramatic change. On quite a few occasions I arrived at a potential inn only to find that it was now a Chinese restaurant, nursing home, that it had been converted into offices or flats, or even that it had been demolished. Multinational conglomerates that install a salaried manager have swallowed up many of the inns that were formerly family concerns, kept by a single tenant for many years, or passed down through successive generations. These modern managers might hold their position for only a year or two before being replaced. In this way, the old traditions and stories – once the stock in trade of the innkeeper – are rapidly being forgotten.

Even that 'reliable' source of information for all ghost and folklore researchers, the knowledgeable local, is being driven from his seat at the bar by an industry more intent on pouring vast quantities of alco-pops down the throats of sweet-toothed clientele than on preserving an important part of our heritage. I would urge those who might accuse me of exaggeration to visit half a dozen or so of the modern heritage industry's pubs, to see for yourselves how virtually every interior is the same, furnished and decorated from a blueprint that the marketing department believes to be everyone's image of a so-called 'traditional' inn. It is for this reason that several famous haunted inns have been omitted from this book; they were so disappointing that I couldn't summon up any enthusiasm for them.

However, gradually my researches began to reap rewards and I managed to find a reasonable selection of inns that were both haunted and characterful. I took the opportunity to revisit some of my old favourites, such as The Skirrid Mountain Inn in Wales, The Goat Gap Inn in Yorkshire and The Crown Hotel in Suffolk. It was also very refreshing to encounter the occasional host who embodied all that an innkeeper should be: a character. I won't name the inn where the landlord threatened to have me arrested for photographing the exterior of his pub before he was actually open! Nor the manager who, in a delightful reversal of the 'How can I help you and have a nice day' ethos of the modern service industry, responded to a request for a cup of tea from an unassuming lady with the straight-faced classic, 'No, madam – this is a public house, *not* a café.'

As it transpired, both of these happened to be haunted pubs and thus are included in the pages that follow. They are among the 130 or so inns that appealed to me on account of their ghost stories and ambience. Inevitably a book such as this becomes a very personal collection, but I sincerely believe that the places included will appeal to you as much as they did to me. And who knows, you might be enjoying a pint by the inglenook one evening, or snuggling beneath the duvet in a low-beamed bedroom, when a sudden drop in temperature, followed by a faint flicker of something mysterious, heralds the approach of a resident wraith ... and you too might be fortunate enough to be able to tell people about the night you saw a ghost!

RICHARD JONES
www.Haunted-Britain.com

THE SOUTH WEST
CORNWALL, DEVON & SOMERSET

The Punch Bowl Inn, Lanreath, Looe, Cornwall – see page 12

The soul of the vicar rose from his lifeless body in the shape of a fearsome black cockerel that terrorized the village.

The West of England is an area steeped in mystery and legend, and the pubs that dot its beautiful and diverse landscapes reflect this aura of enchantment: from the grey-walled hostelries of the wilder reaches of Cornwall, to the pleasant inns nestling in the lovely, lonely villages clinging to the flanks of Dartmoor, and on to pastoral Somerset, where thatched and timbered pubs snuggle harmoniously into the rolling green countryside. The hauntings at these inns are as varied as the scenery around them. There are ghostly monks, mysterious Victorian ladies and murdered soldiers, as well as a fair smattering of regular poltergeist activity. It was on this leg of my journey that I discovered what I consider to be one of the most unique pubs in England, The Highwayman Inn at Sourton: it was like stumbling upon Hansel and Gretel's cottage! The Choughs Hotel at Chard was also a real find, as was The Crumplehorn Inn at Polperro. And it was good to pay another visit to The George and Pilgrim in Glastonbury, a town of which I never tire – if only because of the many residents who have yet to escape from the 1960s!

1. The Dolphin Tavern
2. The St Kew Inn
3. The Crumplehorn Inn and Mill
4. The Punch Bowl Inn
5. The Wellington Hotel
6. Jamaica Inn
7. The New Inn
8. Waterman's Arms
9. The Highwayman Inn
10. The Three Crowns Hotel
11. The Royal Castle Hotel
12. The Smugglers Haunt Hotel
13. The George and Pilgrim Hotel
14. The Choughs Hotel

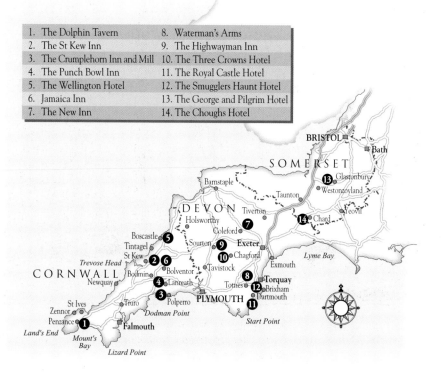

THE DOLPHIN TAVERN
The shade of a Victorian lady

THE DOLPHIN TAVERN ⊨⊀
QUAY STREET
PENZANCE, CORNWALL
TEL: 01736 364106

The Dolphin Inn has echoed to the salty banter of the seafaring fraternity for nigh on 500 years. It is said that the great Elizabethan sailor Sir John Hawkins used it as his base to recruit and organize the Cornish fleet that fought the Spanish Armada in the late 16th century. Later, tradition maintains, the plumes from the first tobacco to be smoked in England wafted among its rafters. Later still the psychopathic Judge Jeffreys is reputed to have turned The Dolphin's dining room into a courtroom, and its cellar into a jail, when he came west to mete out savage retribution against those who had supported the Duke of Monmouth's ill-fated attempt to wrest the throne of England from James II in 1685.

The inn's proximity to the ocean led to frequent flooding over the years, a problem that was finally solved in the mid 19th century when the massive grey seawalls that tower above it were built. It was about this time that the then proprietor, William Pascoe, was fined for refusing to billet soldiers at The Dolphin. His successor, Mr Patch, was not so choosy about his clientele and, in 1868, found himself hauled before the authorities for harbouring lewd and loose women on the premises. But by the early 20th century the hostelry had settled into a respectable old age, and was a favoured stopover for the gentry awaiting the ships that would depart from the harbour opposite, bound for the nearby Isles of Scilly.

At least three ghosts are known to reside within The Dolphin's history-steeped walls. The most persistent is that of an old sea captain who wears a tri-cornered hat, lace ruffles and a striking jacket, resplendent with shiny brass buttons. Successive landlords have come to know him as George, and have been happy to allow him to continue his nefarious wanderings until he tires of plodding about the upstairs rooms and corridors in the dead of night.

Another ghost is that of a woman in Victorian dress, who flits across the main bar much to the surprise of startled onlookers. One Sunday morning in October 2000 a member of staff was sitting at the bar awaiting the start of the busy lunchtime session when the ghost suddenly materialized from the wall beside him and drifted across to the opposite wall, where she simply melted into the stonework.

The final phantom is that of a fair-haired young man. Over the years several landlords and landladies have awoken to find him standing beside, or even sitting on, the end of their beds. No one has ever discovered his identity, for he has the annoying habit of simply melting away the moment anyone speaks to him.

THE ST KEW INN
The girl beneath the floor

The St Kew Inn is one of just a handful of buildings that make up the tiny village of St Kew. It was first licensed in the 18th century, although the building is much older and dates from the 1600s. It boasts a huge open kitchen range and a slate

THE ST KEW INN ✗
CHURCH TOWN, NR BODMIN
ST KEW, CORNWALL
TEL: 01208 841259

floor, one section of which (now covered by concrete) presents visitors with a tantalizing enigma to mull over.

In the 1970s a new water pipe was being laid in the bar, when, in the course of excavations, workmen uncovered the skeleton of a teenage girl. According to forensic experts she had been there for the best part of 100 years, yet no one could discover her identity or find any reason for her decidedly unconventional resting place. She was reburied in consecrated ground, and the spot where she had lain was covered with a concrete slab. But her spirit has chosen to remain at the place of her original interment, and staff and regulars have given her the name 'Adele'. Given that it was building work that led to her re-emergence, it is perhaps fitting that she only appears when alterations are being carried out at the inn. On these occasions people have been known to feel a cold sensation as her invisible form brushes past them. Occasionally witnesses have been treated to a full-fledged spectral apparition, as Adele's sombre shade glides silently by, her unblinking eyes fixed on some distant goal. She tends to evoke affection rather than fear, and is now more or less accepted as the inn's oldest resident.

THE CRUMPLEHORN INN AND MILL
The invisible lovers

Although only an inn since 1972, the attractive group of buildings comprising the The Crumplehorn Inn and Mill are far older, and have had

THE CRUMPLEHORN INN AND MILL 🛏 ✗
POLPERRO, CORNWALL
TEL: 01503 272348

ample opportunity to acquire a few otherworldly residents. In the bar, witnesses speak of an indistinct 'something' glimpsed out of the corner of the eye, but which disappears when they turn to look at it.

Late one Sunday night a barmaid had turned the lights off at the end of her shift and was walking past the toilet when suddenly the door creaked wide open. Thinking she had locked someone in, she shouted an apology, only to be left in disbelief as the door promptly closed again. Mystified, she went to investigate, but found that the toilet was empty.

The inn's owner, Andrew Taylor, has encountered the wraiths that haunt the property on several occasions. His accommodation is situated in the 16th-century mill house. One morning he awoke to see someone standing in front of the mirror, holding a cigarette and clasping their hand to their forehead 'as though they had a really bad headache'. Thinking it must be his wife, Ann, he asked if she was all right. But then he saw that Ann was still in bed beside him. When he looked back towards the mirror the figure had gone.

Andrew is uncertain as to whether the mysterious figure was associated with the other phenomena that he and Ann had experienced. Sometimes, lying in bed late at night, they would hear the voices of a man and woman whispering in the loft above them. On one occasion they even heard the sound of a door latching, although there is no door in the loft! Ann, who sadly died in 1994, was very psychic and formed the impression that the male voice belonged to a World War I soldier who had deserted and was hiding in the loft of the old mill. The female voice was that of his lady-love. Eventually he was captured and sent back to the front where he was killed in the trenches; but it seems that every so often the revenants of the two lovers return to the place where they shared their last moments together.

THE PUNCH BOWL INN
The ghostly cockerel

THE PUNCH BOWL INN ✗
LANREATH
LOOE, CORNWALL
TEL: 01503 220218

The Punch Bowl Inn, in the lovely village of Lanreath, is the keeper of a delightfully melodramatic ghostly tale. The story goes that the parish's old rector was entertaining his curate to dinner one night when the wine ran dry. He headed down to the cellar to fetch another bottle, but tripped on the top stair and tumbled to his death. Some say that the curate, who was having an affair with the rector's wife, pushed him. Whether it was murder or an accident, the next day the vicar returned to haunt the village in the guise of a large black cockerel that attacked anyone who crossed its path. As the villagers cowered indoors, afraid to venture out, the demonic bird flew in through a pub window and into an earthenware oven. The kitchen maid promptly slammed the door shut. To ensure that the fearsome bird stayed put, the landlord summoned a mason who cemented over the oven, thus imprisoning the vicar's vengeful spirit for eternity.

THE WELLINGTON HOTEL
They walk through the walls

Victor Tobutt, owner of Boscastle's 16th-century coaching inn, The Wellington Hotel, was working behind reception one day when a man dressed in a frilly shirt, a frock coat, leather gaiters and boots, his hair tied back in the manner of an 18th-

THE WELLINGTON HOTEL 🛏 ✕
THE HARBOUR
BOSCASTLE, CORNWALL
TEL: 01840 250202

century coachman, drifted slowly past. 'There was nothing insubstantial about him,' Victor later recalled, 'he looked remarkably solid.' However, Victor's mystification turned to shock when the figure promptly disappeared into a solid wall. On discussing his experience with members of staff, Victor learnt that many of them had also encountered this particular ghostly figure, although nobody knew who he was, or why his ghost should roam The Wellington.

Equally mysterious is the misty, cloaked figure that has been seen to emerge from a solid wall on an upstairs landing and drift in front of bemused spectators before vanishing through a closed window. According to tradition, this particular entity is believed to be the ghost of a young girl who, having been crossed in love, flung herself from an upper window of the hotel's tower in despair.

Finally, rooms 9 and 10 of the hotel are the favoured haunts of a little old lady who sits on the beds or walks through the doors, much to the consternation of those who encounter her. Again, her identity remains just one of the many secrets to which a building of such antiquity is inevitably privy. The Wellington Hotel's enigmatic spectral populace appears to be a harmless bunch – and isn't walking through solid walls or locked doors just what ghosts are supposed to do?

JAMAICA INN
The watching phantom

The oldest parts of Jamaica Inn date from the 18th century, and originally it catered for travellers on the new turnpike road from Bodmin to Launceston. Its name came from the local Trelawney family – important

JAMAICA INN 🛏 ✕
BOLVENTOR
LAUNCESTON, CORNWALL
TEL: 01566 86250

landowners in the area, two of whose members served as governors of Jamaica in the 18th century. The surrounding countryside was – and still is – wild, rugged and remote, and the inn gave shelter and sustenance to many a traveller whose weary lot it was to traverse the bleak and windswept sedges of Bodmin Moor. Its wind-lashed walls also provided a haven for less salubrious characters, and for many years it was a notorious haunt of smugglers. The publication in 1936 of Daphne du Maurier's classic novel *Jamaica Inn* made the place famous throughout the world, and led to its expansion into the sprawling tourist complex that greets visitors today.

Several ghosts are said to wander within and around the old hostelry. Phantom footsteps have been heard plodding along corridors at dead of night. The sounds of horses' hooves sometimes clatter over the outside courtyard in the early hours. Witnesses, awoken by the noises, part the curtains to investigate, and see nothing. The murmur of agitated conversation in some foreign tongue, or forgotten dialect, has also been heard in the darker corners of otherwise empty rooms. And every so often, the inn's best-known and oldest ghost transcends the centuries to astonish and bemuse those who chance upon him.

In life he is reputed to have been a wayfarer, who one evening long ago was supping his ale at the bar when a man peered round the door and called for him to come outside. Setting down his half-full tankard, the wayfarer went out into the night and was never seen alive again. The next morning his lifeless corpse was found on Bodmin Moor. His identity and that of his assailant remain a mystery to this day, but his ghost has appeared many times and has a particular attraction to the wall in front of the inn. Here he has often been seen just sitting, silent and motionless. He doesn't respond to greetings, appears oblivious to those who pass by him and, after a few moments of gazing nonchalantly into space, slowly dissolves into nothingness.

THE NEW INN
Death did them part

THE NEW INN 🛏 ✗
COLEFORD
CREDITON, DEVON
TEL: 01363 84242

The New Inn is a spellbinding hostelry, with whitewashed walls, a thatched roof and a history that stretches back to the 13th century. It nestles in a tranquil and pastoral setting, by the babbling waters of a picturesque stream. And this inn even boasts its own resident parrot – the chatty blue-fronted Amazon, 'Captain' – who, at 16 years old, can lay claim to being the inn's third-oldest resident.

Opposite: Cornwall's Jamaica Inn is surrounded by the bleak reaches of Bodmin Moor. A ghostly sailor may well whistle a welcome as you approach!

First in the pecking order is the phantom monk, Sebastian, whose earth-bound wraith has been chilling the marrow of staff and customers alike since long before living memory. According to one version of the story, Sebastian met his fate when he chanced upon a gang of sheep and cattle stealers who were dividing their spoils at the inn. When he threatened to inform on them, the villainous rustlers murdered him.

Another tale, however, depicts Sebastian as having been a lustful friar who embarked upon a passionate affair with a local lady. One night, en route to an illicit liaison, he somehow managed to fall into the stream and was drowned. Whatever the cause of his death, its trauma has caused his ghost to remain behind at the inn, and many guests have felt a cold chill as his invisible shade glides silently past them.

From time to time a female entity has also been seen about the premises, and a male guest even had a brief encounter with her in his room. He was sitting on his bed when he smelt a faint whiff of perfume. Suddenly a glowing light began to form before his very eyes, and he watched, spellbound, as it assumed the indistinct shape of a woman who glided across the room and then disappeared. He later recalled that his experience 'wasn't at all scary – quite pleasant, in fact'. The possibility that the ghost was that of Sebastian's lover coming back for a final phantom fling has been mooted.

WATERMAN'S ARMS
Emily came to stay

WATERMAN'S ARMS 🛏 ✗
BOW BRIDGE
ASHPRINGTON, NR TOTNES, DEVON
TEL: 01803 732214

The Waterman's Arms enjoys a secluded and picturesque riverside location at the head of Bow Creek. It has, over the years, seen service as a smithy, a brewhouse and even a haunt of the dreaded press gangs, who would drag unwilling local lads off to be pressed into service in the navy.

Of course, the Waterman's Arms is also haunted. The melancholic spectre of a grey lady wanders the premises, clutching a bunch of keys. She is known as Emily, and may have been a former lady of the house, or perhaps just a humble serving wench. Nobody knows for sure, and since those whom she honours with her presence do not realize that she is a ghost until she begins 'dissolving' in front of them, she is allowed to wander at will until she chooses to return to whichever dimension and whatever era her journey began.

THE HIGHWAYMAN INN
The West Country's most haunted inn

The Highwayman Inn enjoys a lonely
and dramatic setting. It stands opposite
the pretty little church of St Thomas à
Becket, beyond which the dark bulk of
Dartmoor looms against the scudding
clouds – bleak, brooding and thoroughly

THE HIGHWAYMAN INN 🛏 ✕
SOURTON
NR OAKHAMPTON, DEVON
TEL: 01837 861243

menacing. Until the mid 20th century, this little pub was known as The New
Inn, although it was anything but, since the building dates back to the 13th
century. In 1959 the dilapidated property came into the possession of John
'Buster' Jones, a Welsh visionary whose previous achievements had included
running away to sea when he was 14, and representing Wales at boxing and
distance running. He and his wife, Rita, changed the pub's name to The
Highwayman, and set about transforming the modest roadside watering hole
into one of the most unusual and imaginatively furnished hostelries in the
whole of England.

What Buster Jones created was a fairytale cottage cum Aladdin's cave, with
nautical and ecclesiastical themes thrown in for good measure. He dragged
tree stumps from nearby woodland, and either fashioned them into bar tops
or used them as massive beams to prop up ageing ceilings. The old
Okehampton-to-Launceston stagecoach became a suitably eccentric entrance
lobby. Old spindles, battered tankards, cartwheels, lanterns and all manner of
other bric-à-brac came to occupy every spare inch of wall, beam or ceiling.
Timbers and fittings from old ships – including the intricately carved door of
the whaler *Diana* that ran aground in the Humber in 1869 – were used to
create the remarkable Galleon Bar, which has the below-decks ambience of an
18th-century pirate ship. Buster's daughter, Sally, and her husband, Bruce,
now run the inn and take great care to ensure that his legacy remains intact.
They have long grown used to sharing their bequest with one or two spirits
of an ethereal nature that drop in every so often to keep an eye on the
comings and goings.

Much of the ghostly activity occurs in the Galleon Bar, and it is mooted that
it may be related to the eerie-looking door from the *Diana*. Between
21 September 1866 and 17 March 1868, 13 members of the ship's crew died
when she became trapped in Arctic pack ice. 'We will not have a moment's
peace of mind or body so long as we are in this awful ice,' one sailor wrote in
his log. When the remaining crew finally managed to force the crippled vessel
across the Atlantic to reach Shetland, the first reporter to board her was
appalled by the sight that met his eyes. 'Coleridge's Ancient Mariner might

have sailed in such a ghastly ship,' he wrote, 'the main deck a charnel house not to be described ...'

Several psychic investigators have suggested that the apparitions seen in the Galleon Bar are the long-dead mariners whose spirits have remained earthbound in the fabric of the door. Such a theory might sound a little far-fetched, but a definite air of melancholy emanates from the relic.

Other phenomena experienced here have included items being moved around by invisible hands, orbs of light hovering in mid air, and a ghostly figure in a feathered cap who drifts silently around, no doubt content to roam the eclectic interior of such a characterful and hospitable place.

THE THREE CROWNS HOTEL
The ghostly cavalier

The Three Crowns Hotel dates back to the 13th century. For several hundred years it was the family home of the Whiddons, one of whom, Mary, achieved local notoriety in 1641 when she was shot dead on the

THE THREE CROWNS HOTEL 🛏 ✗
HIGH STREET, CHAGFORD
NEWTON ABBOT, DEVON
TEL: 01647 433444

church steps on her wedding day. No sooner had the village recovered from this tragedy than, two years later, the young Royalist poet Sidney Godolphin was caught up in a local Civil War skirmish and, riddled by musket fire, was carried to what is now the hotel's porch where he died in agony.

Time moved on and the ancient property evolved into a charming old-world inn, its solid granite walls, splendid mullioned windows, massive oak beams and huge fireplace being complemented by, of course, a resident ghost, said to be the sombre shade of the tragic Sidney Godolphin. He wanders the hotel's cosy interior resplendent in full cavalier dress and sporting a handsome plumed hat. He makes fleeting appearances, occasionally startling witnesses by suddenly manifesting in front of them and fixing them with a sad stare. Some who see the ghost of Sidney Godolphin describe him as more melancholic than melevolent. Others who encounter him are moved to admiration by his *pièce de résistance* of walking through granite walls that are so thick that, even though he is a ghost, the feat of passing through them is little short of miraculous!

Opposite: The Highwayman Inn at Sourton is one of the most unusual inns in England and the ambience of its Galleon Bar is greatly enhanced by the chance of an encounter with its ghost.

THE ROYAL CASTLE HOTEL
The phantom coach

THE ROYAL CASTLE HOTEL 🛏 ✕
DARTMOUTH, DEVON
TEL: 01803 833033

The white, castellated façade of The Royal Castle Hotel gazes out across the shimmering waters of the River Dart. Inside there is a veritable time capsule of ancient panelling, beams of hand-hewn timber, some of which was reputedly salvaged from the wood of a wrecked Spanish Armada vessel.

Many famous historical figures have visited the hotel, including Queen Victoria, Edward VII, Sir Francis Drake and Cary Grant. It is also rumoured that several of Charles II's mistresses were sent into polite retirement here.

The great winding staircase, undoubtedly the hotel's most commanding feature, rises from what was the original courtyard. Here the sounds of a phantom coach and horses are sometimes heard in the early hours of autumn mornings. It was at this time of year, in 1688, that William and Mary, following the flight into exile of James II, headed for England from The Netherlands in order to claim the throne. Mary arrived in England first and lodged at The Royal Castle. William had intended to land at Dartmouth, but a storm in the Channel forced him to put in at nearby Torbay instead. A coach, despatched to collect Mary, arrived at The Royal Castle shortly before 2 a.m. – and its phantom has continued to do so ever since.

Guests and staff have frequently been roused by the sound of horses' hooves clattering over cobblestones. Footsteps are heard, followed by a carriage door being opened and then slammed shut. There comes the crack of a whip, the whinnying of horses, and the phantom coach thunders off into the night, its passing always marked by the sound of an invisible clock chiming twice in the street behind the hotel.

THE SMUGGLERS HAUNT HOTEL
Aggie's tumble into the hereafter

THE SMUGGLERS HAUNT HOTEL 🛏 ✕
CHURCH HILL
BRIXHAM, DEVON
TEL: 01803 853050

The Smugglers Haunt Hotel provided me with a delightful conundrum as I set about researching its ghostly occupants. Chris Hudson, the manager, told me that I might like to contact the Torquay police who, apparently, had its ghostly happenings on file.

Intrigued, I duly phoned the Devon and Cornwall Constabulary and asked if it might be possible to view the file. The operator patiently explained that in order to see a file I must go through Data Protection, and connected me with a lady who was most interested in my 'unusual request'. My query, however, posed a little problem since 'technically, Data Protection only protects the living', and so, officially, ghosts do not come under its remit. Since the resources of the Devon and Cornwall Constabulary are more focussed on the activities of the living than the dead, I was left to piece together the hauntings of The Smugglers Haunt from local folklore.

One of the more intriguing characters who over the years has been associated with this 300-year-old inn was Bob Elliot, an infamous Devonshire smuggler who lived in one of two cottages that have now been absorbed into The Smugglers Haunt.

In 1851 Bob and his motley crew were being sought by the excisemen in connection with 142 bales of contraband tobacco. As it so happened, the area that is now the hotel's reception was then inhabited by a coffin maker, and Bob used this opportunity to devise an ingenious method of evading the customs officers when they came looking for him. He put out the news of his own tragic demise and had himself placed inside a large coffin and carried from the premises in solemn procession. He was duly buried in the local churchyard and, once the mourners had left, exhumed by his friends so that he was able to make good his escape. However, Bob's plan very nearly came unstuck when, later that day, he was spotted by three coastguards on their way home from Totnes. Luckily for Bob, they believed him to be a ghost and fled the scene in terror. From that day on he was known as 'Resurrection Bob'.

Unfortunately, Bob's is not one of the two ghosts that are known to reside at The Smugglers Haunt Hotel. Indeed, despite the hotel's name, neither of its revenants is that of a smuggler. The first and most persistent of the resident wraiths is that of a young girl who fell to her death from an upstairs window at a time generally agreed to have been 'around the 1920s'. She is known by staff simply as 'Aggie' (or sometimes 'our Aggie'), and her mischievous spirit often disturbs those who sleep in the room from which she took her tumble by tugging the bedclothes off the bed in the middle of the night.

The Smugglers Haunt's second ghost is a phantom said to be aged about 40, who wears an ankle-length raincoat, sports a flat cap and always appears sitting at a particular table in the bar. Evidently he enjoys the hospitality, and since he bothers no one, the management is more than happy to simply let him be.

THE GEORGE AND PILGRIM HOTEL
Haunted hospitality

THE GEORGE AND PILGRIM HOTEL ⊨ ✕
HIGH STREET
GLASTONBURY, SOMERSET
TEL: 01458 831146

Glastonbury has been dubbed the 'occult capital of England'. On the High Street stands The George and Pilgrim Hotel, built in 1475 to provide hospitality for visitors to the nearby abbey. Its superlative freestone façade and mullioned windows conceal a veritable time capsule with low-beamed, narrow corridors and a winding old stone staircase. And, of course, it has at least two ghosts.

The first is a spectral monk, who has been seen flitting about the dark corridors in the early hours of the morning when the silence is broken only by the creaking of the hotel's ancient timbers.

The second is an elegant lady who sometimes follows him on his nocturnal wanderings with a look of longing admiration upon her pale, emaciated face.

A regular guest at the hotel is a German medium who has told the manageress that the two were lovers in the days of the abbey. Because of the monk's vow of celibacy, theirs was an unconsummated love, the frustration of which has left their spirits forever earthbound and doomed to wander the corridors and passages of The George and Pilgrim.

THE CHOUGHS HOTEL
A ghostly knight and a spectral whipper

THE CHOUGHS HOTEL ⊨ ✕
THE HIGH STREET
CHARD, SOMERSET
TEL: 01460 63266

A rich array of phantoms inhabits the 16th-century Choughs Hotel in Chard. It is a mysterious building of solid stone, riddled with secret passageways, hidden rooms, period furnishings and dark timbers. Set into the wall of an ancient fireplace is what appears to be an inverted tombstone, on which can be discerned a weathered inscription that looks like the name 'Winifred'. It is said that anybody who attempts to take a picture of this mysterious relic using flash photography is destined to fail. The most sophisticated camera equipment has been known to malfunction and, even if the flash does go off, the resulting images are either very foggy or do not appear on the negative at all. Successive landlords have grown used to explaining the anomaly to prospective photographers with the warning, 'The ghost won't like it!'

No one is certain which ghost is responsible for the phenomenon and, since there are several to choose from, the would-be ghost-hunter might be better rewarded seeking out a spectral rather than a photographic image.

A former landlady was walking along an upstairs corridor one night when she encountered the mysterious figure of a knight in armour. His bulk was blocking the passageway, and she thought at first that he must be something to do with the carnival that was taking place in the town that day. She asked him politely if he would mind moving aside to enable her to pass and was nonplussed when he simply vanished.

The ghost of a sinister-looking old man has also been seen crouched by the fireplace in the bar. Some say that this particular entity is that of Judge Jeffreys (see page 10), who supposedly stayed at The Choughs in a room where his coat of arms can still be seen in bas-relief on the wall.

In the early 20th century, a guest at the hotel was awoken one night by the sound of a woman's voice, alternating between whispering and laughing. It was accompanied by the more forceful and menacing voice of a man who appeared to be remonstrating with her. As the strange sound ceased, the guest fell asleep. But next morning he awoke to find a deep red welt across his face, as though a whip had struck him. Not surprisingly, he quickly paid his bill and departed.

Ethereal figures drifting about the hotel, objects that move of their own accord, and doors that slam in the night, are just some of the other supernatural occurrences that give The Choughs a genuine air of antiquated mystery. Those who come here seeking the ambience of old England will not be disappointed.

THE SOUTH

DORSET, WILTSHIRE & HAMPSHIRE

The Eclipse Inn, Winchester, Hampshire – see page 33

Dame Alice Lisle returns to sit silently in the dark recesses of the tavern where she spent her last night.

The landscape of this part of southern England is dominated by the chalklands of Salisbury Plain. It is notable for its impressive white horses and other hill figures, as well as for the great monument Stonehenge. At Avebury can be found the only inn in the world to stand within the bounds of a prehistoric stone circle: The Red Lion. Needless to say, as well as being a very spiritual place, it is also very haunted, and I carry fond memories of the night I spent locked on its upper floors! The inns hereabouts occupy an intriguing mix of locations. The Anchor Inn at Seatown is in as isolated a setting as you could wish for, while, by contrast, The Black Swan Hotel at Devizes is situated on the busy market square, although its wonderful, cosy ambience belies the fact that it is one of the region's most haunted inns. Meanwhile, one of the most picturesque hostelries, The Waggon and Horses, sits beside a busy main road at Beckhampton. Charles Dickens was so taken with it that he wrote his own spooky tale to complement the inn's resident ghosts. An exploration of this part of the country will reward the intrepid ghost-hunter, but it will also appeal to anyone searching for 'olde' England.

1. The Anchor Inn
2. The Royal Lion Hotel
3. The Crown Hotel
4. The Old Bell Hotel
5. The Black Swan Hotel
6. The Waggon and Horses
7. The Red Lion Inn
8. The Crown Hotel
9. The Eclipse Inn
10. The Dolphin Hotel
11. The White Hart Hotel

THE ANCHOR INN
The ghostly exciseman

THE ANCHOR INN 🛏️✕
BRIDPORT
SEATOWN, DORSET
TEL: 01279 489215

The road that runs through Seatown ends abruptly at the 18th-century Anchor Inn, which sits almost on the beach and cowers beneath Golden Cap, the highest point on the south coast. The cove below the inn was an ideal spot for smugglers, and such was the extent of their nefarious activities that, in 1750, it was deemed that Seatown should be given a resident exciseman. From his guardhouse in the village, the unfortunate holder of the post was expected to single-handedly curb the activities of the smugglers. Of course, it proved a thankless task, its impossibility compounded by the fact that the local squire was reputedly the leader of one of the smuggling bands.

The excisemen encountered frequent and open hostility, and one of their number was even shot dead at the top of The Anchor's stairs as he eavesdropped on a group of smugglers in the bar below. His ghost is said still to wander the premises, a sad and forlorn figure condemned to lament the lack of manpower that resulted in his demise.

Supernatural activity, however, is not confined only to the timeless interior of The Anchor. An old cottage that stands next to the inn was once let out for holiday accommodation. Several visitors who stayed there were subjected to close encounters of an ethereal kind, and several of them found their experience so alarming that they refused point-blank to go anywhere near the cottage again!

THE ROYAL LION HOTEL
Phantom footsteps and a chilling encounter

THE ROYAL LION HOTEL 🛏️✕
BROAD STREET
LYME REGIS, DORSET
TEL: 01297 445859

In the Middle Ages, Lyme was an extremely busy port. Indeed, the first clash between Sir Francis Drake's fleet and the Spanish Armada took place in Lyme Bay in 1588. It was also here that James, Duke of Monmouth – leader of the Monmouth Rebellion – landed in 1685. Later, Jane Austen used the town as a setting in her novel *Persuasion*, as did John Fowles in his epic novel *The French Lieutenant's Woman*, the subsequent film of which (starring Jeremy Irons and Meryl Streep) was shot here. Many of Lyme's buildings were used as locations, including The Royal Lion Hotel, a coaching inn that dates back to the beginning of the 17th century – and which also happens to be haunted.

The most disturbing phenomenon encountered at the inn is, without doubt, the cloud of ectoplasm that several witnesses have seen in one of the corridors, and which one woman described as being like a 'damp mist going right through you, turning you to jelly'. People have also heard disembodied footsteps approaching them, and have told how their mystification turns to alarm when, as the invisible form passes by, a chilly sensation envelopes them.

What lies behind these mysterious and unsettling occurrences is not known, although some people believe the fact that public executions were once carried out on the site adjacent to The Royal Lion may have something to do with the unseen revenant that now wanders the corridors of the old hotel.

THE CROWN HOTEL
The ghostly twins whom nobody wanted

The ghosts that haunt The Crown Hotel certainly display a poignant twist of melodrama. Legend holds that in the 17th century deformed twins were born to an owner of the building, and their parents kept them chained in an upstairs

> THE CROWN HOTEL 🛏 ✗
> 25 MARKET STREET
> POOLE, DORSET
> TEL: 01202 672137

room away from the prying eyes of the world outside. Having endured their miserable existence for a while, the poor mites died and were, so tradition claims, buried under the floor of the inn's larder. Their ghosts have since become a more or less permanent ethereal fixture at The Crown, and the sound of children playing has often echoed across the inn's empty courtyard at dead of night.

More substantial is the wraith of a despondent young girl in a white nightdress that has been seen from time to time leaning on a banister. The door of one of the bedrooms has also been known to rattle violently. One guest who experienced it gazed on dumbfounded as the handle then slowly turned and the door creaked open to reveal that no one was outside. Suddenly, he felt a cold chill pass over him; as it did so, a blue light floated from his room, glided down the corridor and melted into the wall. Another guest had to be calmed with a glass of brandy when a man with whom he had been chatting in the toilet had the temerity to suddenly vanish!

THE OLD BELL HOTEL
England's oldest hotel?

THE OLD BELL HOTEL 🛏✕
ABBEY ROW
MALMESBURY, WILTSHIRE
TEL: 01666 822344

The Old Bell was erected around 1220 and has been in continuous use as a place of hospitality ever since. It is a lovely old building, with stone arches, cosy recesses, blazing log fires and a medieval hooded fireplace that was rediscovered as recently as 1986. It was originally used to lodge important guests who came to visit Malmesbury Abbey, next to which the old hostelry stands. The building was greatly expanded in 1908 by its then owner, Joseph Moore. Tradition holds that he financed the project with a cache of gold that he found buried in the grounds of the abbey.

The building is the haunt of a ghostly grey lady, who is sometimes seen drifting around the upper floors in the early hours. Nobody knows who she was, or what indignity or tragedy caused her to remain earthbound. Nor is anyone ever likely to find out: she is a shy spectre who, in a neat reversal of custom, appears to take fright when she meets a living soul, and vanishes into thin air!

THE BLACK SWAN HOTEL
The region's most haunted hotel?

THE BLACK SWAN HOTEL 🛏✕
MARKET PLACE
DEVIZES, WILTSHIRE
TEL: 01380 723259

The Black Swan overlooks the Market Place in Devizes, and although the existing building dates only from 1737, there has been a hostelry on the site for much longer. Indeed, the hotel's brick cellar may well date from the early 17th century. This is, without doubt, one of the spookiest parts of the inn and, as such, has become something of a magnet to investigators of the paranormal in recent years. The results of their researches seldom disappoint. Tape recorders pick up strange knocks and bangs. Thermometers display alarming drops in temperature. Video footage shows orbs of light moving in the darkness, and one intrepid group of ghost-hunters even managed to photograph the image of a face peering at them from the cellar wall.

The thought of spending a night in a cold cellar might not be everyone's idea of a restful break. So for those who prefer their creature comforts and seek a decent night's *unrest* in a haunted bedroom, room 4 is the place to lay your head. Several guests have left this room in the middle of the night when the resident revenant has turned up to interrupt their slumber. She is said to be a young woman in a flowing dress who materializes from the wall, glides to the chair by the window and sits down, gazing out into the night. Having kept her weary vigil for a short time, she rises slowly into the air and floats across to melt into the wall behind the bed. Two researchers who spent a night in the room, hoping to make the acquaintance of the mysterious woman, had what they thought was an incident-free ghost-watching session; until, that is, they watched the film from their video camera that had been trained on the chair all night. At around 1.15 a.m. a misty form could be seen floating in the vicinity of the chair. It is debatable as to whether or not this was the ghostly resident playing to the gallery, but one thing is certain: her frequent visits, coupled with the other phenomena that have been experienced elsewhere in the building, make a visit to The Black Swan a must for all who seek a much-researched and well-documented haunted hostelry.

THE WAGGON AND HORSES
A Dickensian ghost story

With its thick walls of ragged stone, dark windows and thatched roof, The Waggon and Horses looks every bit the cosy inn of yesteryear. Originally it provided for the needs of wagoners whose huge vehicles

> THE WAGGON AND HORSES ✕
> BECKHAMPTON, WILTSHIRE
> TEL: 01672 539418

trundled along the rutted roads of 16th-century Wiltshire. In time it evolved into a coaching inn, and acquired an admirer in the form of none other than Charles Dickens, who was so taken with its convivial ambience that he made it the setting for a ghostly little tale in *Pickwick Papers.*

The story in question, 'The Bagman's Tale', concerns Tom Smart, a commercial traveller who, having driven his gig across Marlborough Downs one storm-tossed night, sought shelter at the inn. 'It was a strange old place built of a kind of shingle ... and [with] a low door with a dark porch.' Tom Smart was partial to hot punch, and having imbibed several glasses became somewhat enamoured with the pub's landlady, 'a buxom widow ... with a face as comfortable as the bar'. Sadly, a tall, dark stranger was likewise smitten, and it was to his attentions that the widow was responding.

At length, Tom was shown to his bedroom, where his attention was drawn to a 'strange, grim-looking high-backed chair, carved in the most fantastic manner'. Something about the chair prevented him from sleeping, and he was astonished when it began to transmogrify into a shrivelled, ugly old man who began winking and leering at him. Tom challenged his strange visitor, demanding to know his business. The ghost informed him that he was the landlady's guardian, and had come back to save her from the clutches of the tall, dark stranger, who was, the old man insisted, already married. As proof, he pointed to an oaken-press and told Tom that, 'in the right-hand pocket of a pair of trousers in that press, he has left a letter, entreating him to return to his disconsolate wife with six ... babes, and all of them small'. So saying, the old man disappeared.

Tom awoke next morning to find that the chair was a chair once more. But, having searched the press, he found the letter, just as the ghost had foretold, and showed it to the landlady. She rebuffed the stranger and, in time, she and Tom were married. As for the chair, 'it was observed to creak very much on the day of the wedding: but Tom Smart could never say for certain whether it was with pleasure or bodily infirmity'.

The real ghosts at The Waggon and Horses have their spectral work cut out to compete with such a dramatic fictional tale, but several have tried! There is, for example, the white-haired old woman who sits at the corner of the bar, casting a concerned eye towards the door. She is said to be the ghost of a former landlady who, determined not to let a little thing like death stand in her way, still likes to welcome customers to *her* inn. The tack room, where the wagoners used to store their tack on grilles that are still visible on the walls, was reputedly where a nun once committed suicide. Her spirit still hangs round the room.

The landlord is more than happy to let his motley crew of phantoms go about their ethereal existence unmolested. 'I made a deal with the ghosts a long time ago,' he says. 'I don't bother them – and they don't bother me.'

THE RED LION INN
Murder, mayhem and three stone circles

THE RED LION INN 🛏 ✕
HIGH STREET, AVEBURY
MARLBOROUGH, WILTSHIRE
TEL: 01672 539266

Many is the landlord and landlady who tries to dream up a unique selling point that will tempt customers over the threshold and thus swell the coffers of their inn. The battle to proclaim theirs the oldest hostelry in England is a well-known ploy, as are the plethora of ghostly inhabitants said to lurk in the darker recesses of many an historic watering hole. None, however, can come close to matching that of The Red Lion, which can claim, without fear of

Opposite: Avebury's Red Lion is the only inn in the world to stand within a prehistoric stone circle. No wonder it's one of Wiltshire's most mysterious hostelries.

contradiction, to be the only inn in the world that is located inside a prehistoric stone circle.

Avebury dates from between 4000 and 2400BC, and is actually made up of three stone circles. The whitewashed walls and dark, thatched roof of The Red Lion provide a strange contrast to the colossal stones that encircle it. The building dates back to the early 1600s, and was a farmhouse until 1802, when it acquired a licence and became a coaching inn. It has done sterling work ever since, attending to the needs of weary travellers and, of late, to those who venture to this legend-shrouded location to experience its aura of mystery.

Several ghosts are known to reside both within and without the ancient property. Very occasionally a phantom carriage, drawn by ghostly horses, has been seen clattering across the inn's courtyard. Successive landlords have preferred not to become acquainted with this spectral visitor, since it is a harbinger of tragedy, and means that a close relative is about to die.

Less traumatic, though equally alarming, is The Red Lion's female phantom, Florrie. During the 17th-century English Civil War, Florrie's husband is said to have returned unannounced from the conflict and caught his wife in the arms of another man. He shot her lover dead and slit his wife's throat. He then dragged her body to the well (still to be seen in one of the pub's front rooms) and, having thrown her down it, sealed it with a huge boulder. Florrie's ghost has remained behind ever since, searching, it is said, for a man with a beard – although whether he represents her husband or her lover tends to vary with different versions of the story. She has been seen emerging from and disappearing into the old well, which is now glassed over to serve both as a curiosity and as a drinks table. Bearded customers do appear to attract her attention. On one occasion a chandelier in the restaurant suddenly began to spin round at an alarming speed. It turned out that the man sitting directly underneath it sported a bushy beard.

Other parts of the 400-year-old building are also haunted. The ghosts of two children, whom several guests have seen cowering in a corner, haunt the Avenue bedroom. An equally ethereal woman who sits writing at the table, either oblivious to or unconcerned by their evident distress, often accompanies them.

Strange orbs of light hovering in the darkness, weird shadows flickering across walls, and cold spots that have been known to chill the marrow of even the most hardened sceptic are just some of the phenomena experienced at this genuinely atmospheric old inn.

Several guests have been so disturbed by their experiences that they have refused to stay another night. The majority, however, fall under the spell of its ancient corridors and creaking floorboards and, like the pub's manager, Richard Bounds, find it a tranquil and calming place. 'Outside the stone circle,' says Richard, 'I can't sleep at night. But in here I sleep like a log.'

THE CROWN HOTEL
Phantom scratching and a walled-up pooch

In 1967 workmen carrying out renovations at the 15th-century Crown Hotel knocked down a false wall near the original dining-room hearth and came across the skeleton of a dog hidden in a recess. The find appeared to give credence to one of the

THE CROWN HOTEL 🛏 ✗
HIGH STREET
ALTON, HAMPSHIRE
TEL: 01420 84567

inn's more persistent legends, which held that at some stage in its long history, a man had beaten his dog to death against the dining-room chimney breast in a fit of drunken rage. Thereafter, ghostly scratching could often be heard in the vicinity of the fireplace, sometimes accompanied by the sound of whimpering from behind the wall. Dogs brought to the inn would often react to something they could either see or sense in the area of the chimney breast. But the finding of the skeleton has not rendered the haunting redundant, for visitors still enquire about the cause of the strange scuffling and frantic scraping that they swear to have heard near the fireplace.

THE ECLIPSE INN
Dame Alice's last stand

On 2 September 1685, Dame Alice Lisle stepped through an upstairs window of this ancient hostelry, placed her weary head upon a wooden block, and was beheaded. She had been sentenced to death at the infamous Bloody Assizes by

THE ECLIPSE INN ✗
25 THE SQUARE
WINCHESTER, HAMPSHIRE
TEL: 01962 865676

the notorious 'hanging Judge Jeffreys', her crime to have given shelter to two rebels fleeing the bloody aftermath of the Monmouth uprising.

Jeffreys wanted her dragged on a hurdle through the streets of Winchester, and then burnt at the stake. But King James II, fearful of the reaction of the people of Hampshire, commuted her sentence to a simple beheading. And so her last night was spent in an upper room of The Eclipse.

Once the executioner had finished his bloody business, her body was conveyed to its final resting place in Ellingham churchyard. The mournful cortège was followed by hundreds of townsfolk, lamenting her unjust fate. Since then, Dame Alice Lisle has returned time and again to the tavern where she spent her last night, appearing suddenly clothed in a grey woollen dress, watching staff and customers silently from the dark recesses of the bar.

THE DOLPHIN HOTEL
Molly the spectral cleaner

With an impressive Georgian façade that is a famous feature of Southampton's High Street, and a roll call of eminent former guests – including Edward Gibbon (author of *The History of the Decline and Fall of the Roman Empire* and visitor in 1762), William

THE DOLPHIN HOTEL ⬌ ✕
34–35 HIGH STREET
SOUTHAMPTON, HAMPSHIRE
TEL: 01703 339955

Makepeace Thackeray (who wrote some of his novel *Pendennis* here in 1850) and Jane Austen (who attended a ball here and was asked to dance by a 'black-eyed, French officer in regimentals') – The Dolphin Hotel can boast a rich and varied history. A ghost of regular though impeccable habits whose name is – or was – Molly, also haunts it. She was, so it is said, a cleaner who died in mysterious circumstances and now chooses to drift around the premises at around 2 a.m., floating just above the ground and leaving a cold chill behind her.

THE WHITE HART HOTEL
The Green Lady and the transparent man

This 300-year-old coaching inn is the haunt of a number of earthbound spirits. Chief among them is the tall Green Lady, whose phantom form has been seen repeatedly gliding along an upstairs corridor in the dead of night. Whether

THE WHITE HART HOTEL ⬌ ✕
BRIDGE STREET
ANDOVER, HAMPSHIRE
TEL: 01264 352266

she is also responsible for the mysterious footsteps heard in other parts of the old building is unknown.

A second female revenant, described as being less distinct, has also been seen. A male companion, in whose ethereal company she drifts silently past bemused bystanders, sometimes joins her. One witness described them as being 'not quite white, but semi-transparent', and went on to explain how their fleeting appearance had left him feeling 'as if a couple of people had drifted through me'. No one has ever discovered their identities nor, for that matter, uncovered what long-ago event, tragic or otherwise, lies behind their spectral ramblings.

Opposite: Jane Austin and William Makepeace Thackeray are just two of the famous faces to have crossed the threshold of Southampton's Dolphin Hotel. But it is a former cleaner named Molly who haunts it.

THE SOUTH EAST

SURREY, WEST SUSSEX, EAST SUSSEX & KENT

The Ringlestone Inn, Ringlestone Hamlet, Nr Harrietsham, Maidstone, Kent – see page 46

*The ghost of the boy who was hidden inside a wall hurls boots
across the bar in rage.*

This region is rich in history, lore and legend, and boasts a varied abundance of old inns, some of which are haunted. The Mermaid Inn at Rye is every inch the creepy old traditional inn, while The Black Horse in Pluckley is located in a place that has long held the dubious distinction of being the most haunted village in England. Tucked away down leafy lanes and byways that wind through the beautiful countryside you will find white weatherboarded old hostelries, the walls of which seep with atmosphere. Then there are places such as The Angel in Guildford, and The George in Crawley, whose time-worn interiors appear to have changed little since they opened their doors for business hundreds of years ago. Add to all this some of the most stunning countryside in the Home Counties, and you have an area which more than rewards a summer or winter's afternoon of exploration.

1. The George
2. The Angel Posting House and Livery
3. The Royal Oak
4. The George
5. The Queen's Head
6. The Mermaid Inn
7. The Chequers Inn
8. The Black Horse
9. The Ringlestone Inn

THE GEORGE
Beaten by the ghost

THE GEORGE 🍴
45 GUILDFORD STREET
CHERTSEY, SURREY
TEL: 01932 886781

The George is a delightful old place, probably built as a hunting lodge at some stage in the 14th century. It became an inn in the mid 15th century, and in the 500 or so years that have since elapsed has managed to acquire a ghostly lady of unknown identity. The reason that no one knows who she is, or was, is because she never hangs around long enough for anyone to find out!

Many are the times that people have been enjoying a glass or two in the atmospheric bar when the sound of footsteps pacing quickly across the upstairs floor is heard. 'It's her,' someone might cry, and those in the know will make an almighty dash up the stairs in the forlorn hope of catching her; but in vain, for no matter how sprightly their sprint, there is never any sign of the ghostly visitor. However, sometimes a deep indentation is found in the centre of one of the beds upstairs, as if someone (or something) has been sitting there just a few seconds earlier.

Could it be that the entity is enjoying a little spectral sport at the expense of staff and regulars? Having lured them upstairs with the sound of her footsteps, does she settle briefly on a bed and revel in their frustration when they find that, yet again, she has beaten them?

THE ANGEL POSTING HOUSE AND LIVERY
The ghostly poser

THE ANGEL POSTING HOUSE AND LIVERY 🍴
91 THE HIGH STREET
GUILDFORD, SURREY
TEL: 01483 564555

The Angel Posting House and Livery – built on medieval monastic foundations and situated on Guildford's cobbled High Street – is the sort of old hostelry that even a cursory glance tells you *must* be haunted. An old man, who sits nonchalantly by the fireplace in the atmospheric downstairs lounge, is the first of several spectres that guests might encounter.

Opposite: Ascend the stairs of Guildford's Angel Posting House and you enter the realm of the spirits. Long dead soldiers and ghostly voices can guarantee a decent night's unrest.

In March 2003 a group of ghost-hunters who spent a night carrying out a paranormal investigation at the hotel was rather pleased with the results. Of particular interest was the fact that their tape recorder, which had been left running in the hotel's William Moore Room, had succeeded in picking up a ghostly voice.

Many guests claim to have seen the apparition of a soldier standing by the wardrobe in the Freiberg Room, which has a long history of haunted hospitality. In 1969 a woman staying in the room – then called the Prince Imperial's Room – phoned the hotel's receptionist and asked to be moved to another room on account of 'something' supernatural that she had, apparently, seen in the mirror. She was unable to give any further information about her ordeal since the sighting had affected her quite deeply.

However, in January 1970 a man and his wife who were occupying the same room awoke in the night to find the dark-haired, moustachioed image of a middle-aged man, wearing a military uniform, gazing at them from the mirror. On this occasion the ghostly reflection was unusually obliging and remained visible for almost 30 minutes. During this extended sighting the guest regained his nerve and proceeded to pen a sketch of his spectral visitor on a red paper napkin!

THE ROYAL OAK

The phantom in the red-spotted handkerchief

> THE ROYAL OAK ✗
> POOK LANE, EAST LAVANT
> CHICHESTER, WEST SUSSEX
> TEL: 01243 527434

In the 18th and 19th centuries The Royal Oak was a popular haunt of smugglers. It is, therefore, right and proper that the ghost of one of these swarthy brigands should haunt it. The story goes that an exciseman once caught a couple of smugglers in possession of their ill-gotten gains. With nothing to lose – and much to gain – the smugglers didn't hesitate in murdering their would-be captor and disposing of his body in a nearby pond. Their dastardly deed, however, did not go unpunished, for when the forces of law and order caught up with them, they were arrested and hanged at a place near The Royal Oak.

As the noose pulled tight and his life ebbed away, the spirit of one of the bootleggers appears to have made a dash for The Royal Oak, where it has remained in residence ever since. Many times since then, heavy footsteps, plodding across the upstairs floor, have disturbed the night hours at the old pub. And there have been many sightings of a red-bearded, misty figure – its head covered by a spotted handkerchief – sitting at the foot of one of the beds. One landlord who saw the figure walk out of the room in question was so taken aback by the sighting that he later described it as nothing less than a 'most shattering experience'.

THE GEORGE
The gentle giant and the poisoned wine

Its position on what was once the main London-to-Brighton road has made The George a popular stopover for thousands of travellers since it first opened its doors for business in 1615. It was a regular resting place for no less

THE GEORGE ⊠ ✗
HIGH STREET
CRAWLEY, WEST SUSSEX
TEL: 01293 524215

a personage than the Prince Regent, later George IV, as he travelled back and forth during the construction of his Royal Pavilion in Brighton. Smugglers too, it is claimed, found it a useful place to break their journeys and plan their exploits.

Needless to say, with such a venerable antiquity, The George has managed to acquire a resident ghost in the robust shape of one Mark Hueston, a giant of a man who stood 6 feet (2 metres) tall and weighed in at a hefty 18 stone (114 kilograms). No wonder the old floorboards creak whenever he is about! He was, so the story goes, employed as a night watchman shortly after the inn was built. He would patrol the corridors in the early hours, armed with a pistol and cutlass. His presence was guaranteed to deter any would-be thief or burglar, and as a result, the inn enjoyed a modest reputation as a safe lodging place.

Then one night, for reasons unknown, a guest decided to put poison in a bottle of wine and leave it by his bed. One suggestion for the reason behind this bizarre act was that someone had been stealing his wine and he wanted to ensure that they received a just and permanent punishment! What the guest didn't realize was that one of the perks of Hueston's job was that he ate and drank all the leftovers when guests departed, and thus it was Hueston who quaffed the deadly concoction. The next morning, he was found dead in the small cubbyhole that is situated opposite what is now a function room. To this day some people claim that this area of the inn possesses a strange and uneasy aura. Others, meanwhile, claim to see a shapeless apparition here, which is presumed to be Hueston's wraith maintaining his weary vigil, making him as dedicated a night watchman in death as ever he was in life.

THE QUEEN'S HEAD
The landlord who never left

One of the most popular landlords ever to grace the old Queen's Head was George Gustell, who kept it in the latter half of the 19th century. He was so well liked that, when he died in 1890, his customers decided to hold a wake in

| THE QUEEN'S HEAD ✕ |
| PARSONAGE LANE, ICKLESHAM |
| WINCHELSEA, EAST SUSSEX |
| TEL: 01242 814552 |

order to give him a send-off to be proud of. His coffin was brought into the bar and laid upon the counter, and copious amounts of alcohol were consumed in his memory. Everyone agreed that, despite the sadness of the occasion, a good time was had by all.

Even old George seems to have enjoyed it immensely, and has shown a marked reluctance to leave the pub, opting instead to remain behind as an earthbound spirit. His spruce and portly spectre looks anything but the hazy phantom figure of tradition. He sports a fine beard, handsome sideburns and moustache. He wears a rough tweed waistcoat, from the pocket of which dangles a gold watch chain, and his shirtsleeves are rolled up to the elbow. Indeed, so regular were his appearances at The Queen's Head at one stage that a glass of whisky used to be left permanently alongside his favourite chair. But as with many a resident ghost, his appearances are waning, and it seems that the time is fast approaching when his spectral visitations will be little more than a distant, albeit curious, memory.

THE MERMAID INN
The battling spectres

Rye is a delightfully unspoilt town that was a fortified seaport, until the waters began to recede in the 16th century.

Although it is now 2 miles (3.2 kilometres) from the sea, the town still possesses a unique character, and boasts

| THE MERMAID INN ⊨ ✕ |
| MERMAID STREET |
| RYE, EAST SUSSEX |
| TEL: 01797 223065 |

an impressive array of picturesque buildings. One of the largest medieval buildings in the town is The Mermaid Inn, which sits on the steep, narrow and

Opposite: The Mermaid in Rye must be one of the most photographed inns in England. Its interior is ancient and creepy and former residents are still active within its creeper-clad walls.

cobblestoned Mermaid Street. It opened for business in 1420 and it is without doubt one of England's most beautiful inns. Its timeless façade must have adorned more coffee-table books and tourist brochures than any other inn or pub in Britain.

Needless to say, with the scars and emotions of over 500 years of habitation emblazoned upon its ancient timbers – and some of that of a decidedly nefarious nature, such as being used as a base by a ruthless band of smugglers, the Hawkhurst Gang, in the 18th century – The Mermaid can boast of a veritable array of spirits to chill the blood of modern-day visitors. It has acquired that staple of Britain's spectral landscape – its very own grey lady. Indeed, The Mermaid's grey lady so terrified one couple when she appeared at the foot of their bed that they ran downstairs in their night clothes and remained in the lounge till morning. She may be the same grey lady who appears in a chair by the fireplace in room 1, and who somehow manages to soak any clothes that might have been left overnight on that particular chair.

Meanwhile, a man in old-fashioned dress is occasionally seen sitting on the bed in room 18, while room 10 is the spectral domain of a male figure who appears from out of the bathroom wall, walks across the room and then disappears into the wall nearest the bed. A phantom woman, who responds to greetings of 'Good morning' by vanishing, is also encountered in the corridors from time to time.

But perhaps the most famous incident from The Mermaid's ghostly past occurred in the early years of the 20th century when it was being run as a private club by Mrs May Adlington, mother of the novelist Richard Adlington. There had long been reports of a ghost appearing in the building's Elizabethan Chamber on 29 October every year. When, one year, a medium asked to spend that night in that particular room, Mrs Adlington not only agreed to the request, but also offered to keep the woman company. No sooner had they settled down for the night than they both fell fast asleep.

In the early hours, May Adlington awoke to find a pair of phantom duellists, dressed in doublet and hose, battling each other with rapiers. Round and round the room they swirled, thrusting and parrying until one of the combatants inflicted what appeared to be a fatal stab wound upon his foe. As the injured spook slumped to the ground, the victor dragged him across the floor and threw his body into an oubliette – or little dungeon – in the corner of the room. The oubliette has long since been filled in, but the spectral duellists remain. Whoever they may have been in life, in death their antics have helped make them one of the best-known ghostly duos at what is a truly venerable and, in parts, genuinely creepy old hostelry.

THE CHEQUERS INN
The cross-carving phantom

Although The Chequers dates back to the 14th century, it did not acquire its spectral resident until the Napoleonic Wars of the early 1800s. Tradition is divided as to whether the ghost was an English soldier heading home from the wars who was murdered for

THE CHEQUERS INN 🛏️✗
THE STREET
SMARDEN, KENT
TEL: 01233 770217

his pay packet, or a French soldier who had escaped from nearby Sissinghurst Castle and who was caught and killed at the inn. Whatever his nationality and cause of death, his ghost has been heard many times pacing impatiently – some say anxiously – across the inn's upper floor.

Most of the supernatural activity focuses on room 6, where staff have been mystified to find that although the room is empty the bedclothes clearly show a depression, as if someone has been lying on the bed. Dogs have been known to go absolutely wild for no apparent reason, and one poor Afghan hound was so unnerved by the ghostly goings-on that it had to be calmed down with tranquillizers! A woman guest was awoken one night by the chilling sensation of something scratching her back, and her husband later discovered that a small cross had mysteriously appeared on her flesh. Another lady woke in the middle of the night to find the door of her room slowly opening, and she clearly saw a short, dark man standing in the doorway. She shouted out, demanding to know what he wanted, whereupon the figure promptly vanished!

THE BLACK HORSE
A haunted inn in England's most haunted village

Pluckley is widely acknowledged as being the most haunted village in England. Many of the ghosts are connected to the Dering family, Lords of the Manor from the 15th to early 20th centuries. An enduring symbol of their

THE BLACK HORSE ✗
THE STREET, PLUCKLEY
ASHFORD, KENT
TEL: 01233 840256

tenure can be seen in the round-topped windows that grace so many of the buildings. During the Civil War, Lord Dering escaped capture by the Parliamentarians when he dived head first through such a window. When he later came to rebuild his manor house, he commemorated the feat by having every window built in that style, which was copied throughout the village.

The Black Horse Inn began life in the 14th century as a farmhouse and was, for a long time, encircled by a moat. Although this was filled in long ago, traces of it are still discernable. A ghostly prankster who delights in hiding the possessions of staff and customers alike haunts the pub, and he or she has locked managers out on more than one occasion.

One morning in November 1997, landlady Laura Gambling (who had only just taken over the pub) was enjoying a cup of tea prior to opening for her first busy Sunday lunch session, when a glass on the shelf above the bar began to move slightly. She watched in amazement as an unseen hand pushed the glass along the length of the shelf and stopped precariously close to the edge. It seemed as though the ghost was enjoying a little spooky sport by teasing her.

Invisible hands have also been known to lift cutlery from the dresser and arrange them neatly on the side. There is also a spot in the kitchen where dogs will stop abruptly and begin barking at someone, or something, that they can apparently see, but which remains invisible to the human eye.

THE RINGLESTONE INN
The ghost from the cellar

THE RINGLESTONE INN
RINGLESTONE HAMLET, NR HARRIETSHAM
MAIDSTONE, KENT
TEL: 01622 859900

Stepping into the lamp-lit interior of The Ringlestone Inn, you enter a characterful 16th-century farmhouse that has changed little since the day it was built in 1533. The original brick-and-flint walls, ancient floors, old beams, inglenook fireplaces, antique furnishings and tables made from the timbers of an 18th-century Thames barge are quaintly reminiscent of an earlier, less frantic age.

Inevitably, the old building – which has been an alehouse since 1615 – is haunted. Customers have spoken of holding conversations with an elderly couple sitting in two antique chairs in the oldest part of the bar. Mysteriously, if they turn away for a moment, they will look back and find that the chatty seniors have disappeared!

Then there are the ghostly footsteps that, for as long as anyone can remember, have been heard stomping up the stairs from the cellar at dead of night. The unseen revenant pauses on the top step and proceeds to remove an invisible boot which, moments later, is heard clattering across the floor in an apparent fit of phantom pique.

There is a tradition that a young boy once ran away from the army during combat and returned to his home at The Ringlestone. Anxious to avoid him being shot for desertion, his family hid him behind a false wall in the cellar. They left one loose brick through which they would pass food and water. But one day he stopped taking the vitals and, realizing he was dead, his relatives sealed up the loose brick!

Perhaps it is his family's apparent callousness that have spurred his spirit into breaking free from his eternal tomb to ascend the cellar steps, where he shows his indignation by hurling a phantom boot across the room. His bones may even still be lying behind the cellar wall.

No one knows for sure, for as the inn's owner, Michelle Stanley, is happy to point out, 'The cellar has never been investigated and we are none too curious to find out ourselves!

LONDON AND THE HOME COUNTIES

LONDON, BERKSHIRE, BUCKINGHAMSHIRE, BEDFORDSHIRE & HERTFORDSHIRE

The Ostrich Inn, Colnbrook, Slough, Berkshire – see page 53
*Jarman helps another victim to his death, tipping an insensible sleeper
into a vat of boiling fat.*

London is the most haunted capital city in the world, with ghosts that span the centuries and often illuminate gruesome corners of a dark and sinister past. There are so many haunted pubs to choose from that I was almost over-whelmed! However, I opted for two of the capital's most atmospheric and timeless hostelries: The George Inn in Borough High Street, and Hampstead's delightfully rural Spaniards Inn on the edge of Hampstead Heath. One of the great surprises about London is the capital's proximity to beautiful countryside. The Hertfordshire village of Ayot St Lawrence, for example, is only a stone's throw away, yet a more pastoral setting could not be imagined. There are many other rural villages to the north and west of London offering a similar ambience, and the ghosts that haunt their inns tend to reflect this serenity. So, having enjoyed the history-steeped streets of the metropolis, it is well worth heading out into the countryside to discover secluded inns where the hauntings might be less dramatic but are, nonetheless, as intriguing as any in Britain.

1. The George Inn
2. The Spaniards Inn
3. The Bull Hotel
4. The Ostrich Inn
5. The Bull and Butcher
6. The George and Dragon Hotel
7. The Knife and Cleaver
8. The White Hart Inn
9. The Feathers Inn
10. The Brocket Arms

THE GEORGE INN
The formidable phantom of Miss Murray

For centuries, Southwark's Borough
High Street was lined with old coaching
inns. 'Great rambling, queer old places,'
according to Charles Dickens in *Pickwick
Papers,* 'with galleries, and passages, and
staircases, wide enough and antiquated

> THE GEORGE INN ✗
> 77 BOROUGH HIGH STREET
> SOUTHWARK, LONDON
> TEL: 020 7407 2056

enough, to furnish materials for a hundred ghost stories.' Sadly, only one of
them, The George Inn, survived the coming of the railways in the 19th
century, and now enjoys the distinction of being the capital's only galleried
coaching inn.

The George Inn dates from 1677, and as you turn into its cobbled
courtyard you are transported back to another age. From the gallery that
looks down upon the yard, travellers and inn workers once gazed down upon
the coaches as they clattered in through the gates. You can almost hear the
whinnying of horses, the cursing of stablehands and the banter of coachmen.
It comes as little surprise to learn that this gem of bygone London is
haunted.

Several members of staff, who reside on the premises, have been awoken
in the early hours to find the misty form of a woman floating around their
rooms. No one knows for sure who she is, but a likely contender is the
formidable Miss Murray, who kept The George for 50 years in the latter half
of the 19th and early part of the 20th centuries. It was during her tenure that
the coming of the railways sounded the death knell for the coaching age, and
led to the demolition of the neighbouring inns. Three galleries of her
beloved George were also demolished before public outcry saved the
remainder of the building.

Having watched so much of the property fall victim to the voracious
appetite of the new age of horseless transport, Miss Murray's spirit displays
outright antagonism towards modern technology. New tills can be guaranteed
to go wrong. Engineers will be called out time and again to repair them but
can never find any logical explanation. Computers will suddenly crash for no
reason, and digital cameras have often malfunctioned when their owners
have attempted to photograph the interior of what is, without doubt, one of
London's cosiest and most timeless hostelries.

*Opposite: The George Inn in Southwark is a true gem of bygone London. It is
also haunted by a former landlady who is determined to keep the modern
world at bay.*

THE SPANIARDS INN

Black Bess's eternal gallop

THE SPANIARDS INN ✕
SPANIARDS ROAD
HAMPSTEAD, LONDON
TEL: 020 8731 6571

One of the great mysteries surrounding this low-beamed, 16th-century tavern on Hampstead Heath is why its ghostly populace is not swollen by motorists: cars run the risk of a head-on collision at the spot immediately outside where a two-way road suddenly funnels into one narrow lane, on a blind bend!

The inn has an eventful history, and is reputedly named for two Spanish brothers who argued over the love of a woman and then slew each other in a duel. During the Gordon Riots of 1780, the mob, en route to destroy nearby Kenwood House, then home of the Earl of Mansfield, paused at the inn to slake their thirsts. The quick-thinking landlord professed support for their cause and showed and offered them unlimited refreshment. He stalled them long enough for the military to arrive and thus helped save Kenwood for future generations. Later, Charles Dickens was a regular and wrote about the inn in *Pickwick Papers*.

It is, however, a more notorious ex-customer whose ghost haunts the inn. The highwayman and folk hero Dick Turpin is supposed to have stabled his legendary mount, Black Bess, here. Her ghostly hoof beats are said to be heard galloping across the car park at dead of night. Turpin has been seen inside the premises – a shadowy, cloaked figure striding purposefully across the bar and disappearing into a wall. On the first floor is the panelled Turpin's Bar, where a roaring log fire warms visitors in the winter months, and customers have often been startled by an unseen hand that tugs gently at their sleeves.

The Spaniards Inn is a perfect spot to while away the hours. And if your peace is shattered by a loud screech, worry not – it is probably another motorist who has narrowly escaped death on one of London's most precarious bottlenecks.

THE BULL HOTEL

The woman who mourns an indiscretion

THE BULL HOTEL 🛏✕
HIGH STREET
WARGRAVE, BERKSHIRE
TEL: 0118 940 3120

Situated in the heart of Wargrave, the 15th-century Bull Hotel, with its tall chimneys, dark brick walls and complement of bow-fronted windows, exudes a timeless appeal that no amount of contemporary development can subdue. Its interior is cosy and welcoming, with the added comfort of a blazing log fire to warm patrons in the winter months. In the summer you can sit in the walled garden and, as you sup at your pint, keep a keen ear cocked for the faint sound of a woman weeping. Should you hear it, you can take consolation in the fact that you are one of the fortunate few to have heard the ghost.

Tradition holds that the woman whose shade now haunts the old inn was the wife of a 19th-century landlord. Unbeknown to her husband, she had embarked upon a passionate affair. One day, however, her husband caught her *in flagrante* with her lover, and was so incensed that he threw her out and forbade her from returning to The Bull. Maliciously, he also prevented her from ever seeing their infant child again. The poor woman was devastated and, having sunk into melancholy, died shortly afterwards of a broken heart.

It wasn't long before her mournful spectre returned to the pub, and by the dawn of the 20th century it was well known that she haunted room 2. Many people have commented on the creepy atmosphere there. Others say that they often hear the heart-rending sound of a woman weeping in the room, although there is never anybody there when witnesses investigate. Thus it is that the poor woman's ordeal continues, her ghost condemned to relive the moment that her indiscretion came to light and her enraged husband meted out a punishment that even he could not have realized would last for so long.

THE OSTRICH INN
Jarman, the not-so-perfect host

This atmospheric old inn stands in the ancient village of Colnbrook and was once an important stopover on the main stagecoach route from London to Bath. Not wishing to take part in the endless battle to proclaim itself the oldest pub in

THE OSTRICH INN ✗
42 HIGH STREET, COLNBROOK
SLOUGH, BERKSHIRE
TEL: 01753 682628

England, The Ostrich plays it safe and claims to be the 'third oldest'; based on records that date as far back as 1165. One thing it can definitely claim, however, is that it was the first pub in England ever to be featured in a novel – *Thomas of Reading*, written in the late 16th century by Thomas Deloney.

Deloney's reporting of the nefarious exploits of a former landlord, Jarman, secured The Ostrich's place in Berkshire legend. His infamous crimes are generally thought to have taken place around the 1300s. In those days, wealthy travellers would pause at the inn to change from their mud-spattered clothes into the finery expected for their appearances before the monarch at nearby Windsor Castle. Many would often carry vast sums of money – a fact that didn't go unnoticed by Jarman. He soon devised a profitable and intricate method of relieving them of both their riches and their lives.

Whenever an apparently affluent patron arrived at his inn, Jarman would waste no time in plying the stranger with strong drink. Having arranged for these special guests to sleep in his 'best room', he would give them time to collapse into bed and, once certain that they were fast asleep, would undo two bolts on the ceiling in the room beneath. This would cause the bed above to tilt downwards at a 45-degree angle, sending the insensible sleeper tumbling into a vat of boiling fat that Jarman always kept ready in the room below. He would then steal his victim's belongings, sell his horse and clothes to the unquestioning gypsies, and dispose of the body into the nearby river.

Jarman profited immensely from his activities and managed to escape suspicion for many years. Until one night a suitably drunken stranger had crawled into bed only to climb straight back out and make use of the room's chamber pot. As he answered the call, he was astonished to see the head of his bed suddenly tilt and disappear into the floor. His terrified shouts roused the other guests, and Jarman's murderous career was over. On the gallows, Jarman boasted of having killed more than 60 people, although the actual total is believed to be closer to 15.

Staff at the inn are often troubled by the 'sinister atmosphere' that seems to hang over certain sections, and several landlords have complained of their night-time repose being rudely disturbed by the eerie sound of creaking boards, ghostly sighs and spectral bumps, attributed to one of Jarman's hapless victims.

THE BULL AND BUTCHER
Murder, suicide and an untidy ghost

THE BULL AND BUTCHER X
TURVILLE, BUCKINGHAMSHIRE
TEL: 01491 638283

One morning in 1942, P.C. Goldsmith arrived at The Bull and Butcher in the charming Buckinghamshire village of Turville. Propping a ladder against its whitewashed walls, he climbed up to the front bedroom window and, having smashed a pane of glass, let himself in. Once inside, he stumbled upon one of the most gruesome discoveries of his

Opposite: Warm yourself by the fire at Turville's Bull and Butcher, and you might just catch a glimpse of its ghostly landlord, Lacey Beckett.

career. In a pool of blood lay the landlord, Lacey Beckett, with the bodies of his wife and their pet dog nearby. Beckett had left behind a hastily scribbled note asking God's forgiveness for the crime he was about to commit, and from this it was deduced that, having murdered his wife and dog, the landlord had turned the gun on himself. For several months before that fateful day, Lacey Beckett had been complaining of searing headaches. It emerged after his death that these were caused by a brain tumour, and that this probably led to the violence of his final moments.

Today, there is little at this lovely 17th-century inn to recall this isolated and violent incident in its otherwise tranquil past. The village of Turville has a sleepy atmosphere, and on the hillside opposite the inn stands a picturesque windmill that became famous throughout the world when Turville was used as a location during the filming of *Chitty Chitty Bang Bang*. The Bull and Butcher is likewise a star of both large and small screens, and has been featured in several films, as well as in the television series *The Vicar of Dibley*.

But every so often, memories of the tragedy stir within the pub's ancient walls. Landlords have complained of items being moved around on them and, on one occasion, a fastidious barman, who had ensured that the bar was spick and span, left the room for a moment and returned to find the bar towels rearranged untidily. There was even a white powder that had been sprinkled into the newly cleaned ashtrays.

In the past, several locals are said to have seen Lacey Beckett's unmistakable form sitting by the fire in the lounge, and one or two even claimed to have conversed with him, although how long they had been imbibing beforehand is not recorded! Indeed, the spectral landlord was most forthcoming about the reasons for his disruptive behaviour. His wife, he explained, had been an extremely tidy person and he simply could not bear to be reminded of her!

THE GEORGE AND DRAGON HOTEL
Hell hath no fury

THE GEORGE AND DRAGON HOTEL ⬛✖
HIGH STREET
WEST WYCOMBE, BUCKINGHAMSHIRE
TEL: 01494 464414

One of West Wycombe's most infamous sons was Sir Francis Dashwood. He was responsible for excavating the nearby West Wycombe caves for the debauched cavortings of the notorious 'Hell Fire Club', a group of fellow aristocrats and men of influence.

Men from the village were employed in the construction of the caves and were thus saved from the crushing poverty of their age, so earning Dashwood the gratitude of the locals and ensuring that they were willing to turn a blind eye to the spurious goings-on beneath the hillside.

The village today is a delightful enclave, owned and preserved by the National Trust, and a stroll along its High Street is like slipping back in time. The red-brick façade of The George and Dragon is one of the village's more striking exteriors, and turning under its archway to enter its snug and atmospheric interior is a rare treat. 'Generations of traders, travellers, lovers and visitors have left traces of their presence on the building and its atmosphere,' reads the inn's brochure, 'not least of whom is Sukie, the beautiful social climber whose ghost is said to haunt the building.'

Tradition holds that Sukie was a servant girl who worked at The George and Dragon in the 18th century. Among her many admirers were three boys from the village, whose advances she rejected since she had set her sights on becoming the mistress of an aristocrat. One day a wealthy young man paid a visit to the inn and Sukie, seeing him as her ticket out of there, promptly set about ensnaring him. Soon the handsome young buck was besotted with the beautiful servant girl and began paying daily visits to the inn. This irked the three local lads, who hatched a cunning plan to teach the haughty temptress a lesson. They sent her a letter, which purported to come from her noble suitor, informing her that he wished to elope with her. She was, he instructed, to don a white dress and meet him that night in the West Wycombe caves. Elated, the unsuspecting Sukie dressed accordingly and set off for her rendezvous.

Arriving at the mouth of the caves, she lit a flaming torch and entered the labyrinth. Hidden behind a large rock, the spurned lads watched with anticipation as she approached. Just as she had passed by, they seized the torch and dashed it to the ground, extinguishing its flame. Sukie was terrified and fled into the darkness with her whooping tormentors in hot pursuit. It was then that the prank turned to tragedy. As the frightened girl turned a corner, she tripped over a rock and her head struck the cave wall, knocking her unconscious. The three lads summoned help and the villagers arrived to carry the comatose girl back to her room at The George and Dragon. A doctor was called, but in the early hours of the next morning the poor girl died.

It wasn't long before reports were circulating that Sukie's restless wraith was haunting The George and Dragon. The two maids who shared her room were visited by her just a few days after her demise and refused point-blank to set foot in the inn again.

Over the succeeding centuries there were frequent reports of a ghostly white lady seen drifting about The George and Dragon in the early hours of the morning. In 1966, Mr Jhan Robbins, an American guest staying at the hotel, awoke one night to find 'a pinpoint of light glowing about three feet off the ground near the door'. He watched as the light began to grow in stature and took on an 'opaque, pearly quality'. Flinging back the covers he leapt out of bed and strode resolutely towards it. Suddenly he 'entered a zone of intense cold'; his arms and legs became heavy, and he was overcome by a feeling of utter despondency. 'Life seemed futile, beset by tragedy. Life must have felt like this for poor Sukie, I thought, no one to protect her dignity.' At this realization, 'the light ballooned forward and seemed to reach for me'. This proved too much for the, until then, fearless Mr Robbins. He turned off the light and jumped straight back into bed.

Sukie is the best attested of The George and Dragon's ghosts, but she is not alone. Heavy footsteps are often heard descending the main staircase. These are believed to belong to a traveller who was murdered at the inn in the 18th century. His name and the circumstances behind his demise have long since been forgotten, and only the onerous plodding now testifies to the event. Other female phantoms have been seen at various locations around the inn, but Sukie's story and her subsequent nefarious ramblings put them all in the shade.

THE KNIFE AND CLEAVER
The ghost that dogs fear

THE KNIFE AND CLEAVER 🛏️ ✕
THE GROVE
HOUGHTON CONQUEST, BEDFORDSHIRE
TEL: 01234 740387

Although the earliest records for this venerable old hostelry date only from 1796, the building is believed to be much older. It stands opposite the parish church and may well have been built to cater for the needs of ecclesiastical visitors. Its dark-beamed bar is truly atmospheric, and the exquisite Jacobean oak panelling that adorns it is thought to have come from nearby Houghton House, which was stripped of its fixtures and fittings in 1794.

Two ghosts, one male and one female, are known to reside at the pub, but whether they are, or were, related is not known. Landlady Pauline Loom actually saw the male ghost in 1990, and although this was her only sighting, she has sensed his presence many times since. Her pet dog, McCoy, often starts barking quite fiercely at something it can apparently see in one section of the bar, but which remains invisible to humans. The female phantom, though never seen, is most certainly felt, and hardly a day goes by without someone sensing her presence. A student barman once looked on in amazement as the pages of the booking diary began to turn of their own accord. Moments later his astonishment turned to fright when a ghostly hand appeared over his shoulder! He was unable to say which of the two phantoms was responsible, for, quite sensibly, he didn't stick around long enough to find out!

THE WHITE HART INN
Terror on the stairs

Parts of The White Hart date back to the 1530s, although the events that have left an ethereal stain on its ancient fabric date from the 18th century. This was the age when press gangs would arrive at pubs such as

> THE WHITE HART INN ✕
> 30 HIGH STREET
> HEMEL HEMPSTEAD, HERTFORDSHIRE
> TEL: 01442 242458

this to bribe, cajole or even kidnap 'volunteers' to serve in the army or navy.

Legend tells of one unfortunate young man who was supping alone at the bar one night when a group of these recruitment specialists came marching in to The White Hart in search of likely prey. Impressed by his stature, they attempted to convince him that a life in the army was just what he needed. When the lad showed a marked reluctance to join up, they adopted a more persuasive approach, and in the ensuing mêlée, the unfortunate recruit was beaten to death at the foot of the stairs. To this day, customers often complain of experiencing a sensation of sheer terror upon approaching the scene of his demise. There are also reports of agitated voices heard in the empty bar at dead of night, and of the apparition of a scared young man scurrying across the bar, which vanishes in the vicinity of the stairs. The overwhelming feeling of unease that hangs around the area where the tragedy occurred is so intense that several bar staff have flatly refused to go anywhere near the stairs ever again.

THE FEATHERS INN
The tragic wraith of a ghostly girl

Built in the early 1600s, and initially known as The Princes Arms, this old brown-brick hostelry changed its name to The Feathers Inn in 1670, and within 100 years had become one of the area's busiest coaching inns,

> THE FEATHERS INN ⌑ ✕
> CAMBRIDGE ROAD, WADESMILL
> WARE, HERTFORDSHIRE
> TEL: 01920 462606

with stabling for over 100 horses. The section to the right of the bar was once part of the courtyard into which the stagecoaches would come thundering, often at alarming speeds; and woe betide anyone who got in the way of these lumbering great conveyances.

Tradition holds that on one occasion – as is often the case with ghost stories, the date is unspecified and is simply referred to as having been 'centuries ago' – a little girl was playing in the courtyard of the inn, when a London-bound coach came clattering round the corner. Although the coachman saw her, he was unable to bring his horses to a halt in time to save the poor girl from being mown down. They carried her to an upstairs room, but her injuries proved untreatable and she died a few hours later. Many people now catch fleeting glimpses in the corner of the rear right bar where the tragedy is thought to have happened. Witnesses describe her as a small, fair-haired girl, whose face is frozen in terror as her ghost endures the terrible sight of her approaching fate time after time.

THE BROCKET ARMS
The happy monk

THE BROCKET ARMS 🛏 ✗
AYOT ST LAWRENCE
WELWYN, HERTFORDSHIRE
TEL: 01438 820250

Ayot St Lawrence, reached along high-banked lanes, flanked by enormous old trees, is one of the most tranquil and beautiful villages in south-east England. One day, as he was reading the inscriptions on the tombstones in the churchyard, George Bernard Shaw chanced upon the grave of a woman who had died at the age of 70. Its simple epitaph – 'Her time was short' – intrigued him and, observing that any place 'where they call a life of 70 a short one, was the right place for me', he set about moving to this delightful little corner of rural Hertfordshire. It was a wise decision, for he lived to the ripe old age of 94. His house, Shaw's Corner, is now owned by the National Trust, and has long been a place of literary pilgrimage.

There are, however, many reasons for visiting Ayot St Lawrence, and chief among them must be the opportunity to experience the village's picturesque and historic inn, The Brocket Arms. The moment you set eyes on it you know the place is haunted, and this feeling intensifies as you duck into its oak-beamed interior and warm yourself before the blazing log fire that, in winter months, crackles and spits in the massive inglenook fireplace.

The 14th-century Brocket Arms was originally the monastic quarters for the nearby Norman church and it is, therefore, quite natural that its resident ghost should be that of a monk. He is described as a little man in a brown habit whose face is nearly always hidden by a cowl. Sometimes he chooses to appear in a corner of the bar, although he promptly vanishes the moment anyone talks to or even looks at him. Mysterious banging and thumping sounds are often heard coming from upstairs, even though that section is known to be empty at the time. More disturbing are the ghostly slappings of phantom feet that have been known to follow staff down the stairs.

There is a tradition that, in life, the ghostly monk was tried and found guilty of some long-forgotten indiscretion, and executed by being strung up from a beam inside the inn. The truth is that no one knows for sure what trauma lies behind the phantom friar's restless roaming, and since he is, in the words of the landlady, 'an affable character', he is more than welcome to make himself at home.

East Anglia
Essex, Suffolk, Norfolk & Cambridgeshire

The Old Ferry Boat Inn, Nr Holywell, St Ives, Cambridgeshire – see page 72

At midnight, the ghost of Janet Tewslie rises from the granite square in the floor.

Drive eastwards from London and in no time at all the stresses and strains of the modern age fall away, and you find yourself in the rural reaches of Essex, on the threshold of the ancient kingdom of East Anglia. This was the area where, during the anti-witchcraft hysteria of the 16th and 17th centuries, more unfortunates were executed than anywhere else in England. It is therefore fitting that one of the ghosts that we encounter in this chapter should be that of Matthew Hopkins, the self-styled Witch-finder General, who held court at, among other places, Colchester Castle, where there is an exhibition detailing his fanatical excesses. Elsewhere, the tranquil landscape of Suffolk can boast some magnificent haunted inns that stand as proud testimony to the wool-related wealth that this region once enjoyed. Norfolk and Cambridgeshire, meanwhile, can offer some timeless and quaint old hostelries where the ghostly appearances, in one case at least, have become something of an annual fixture.

1. The Red Lion Hotel
2. The Thorn Hotel
3. The Cross Keys Hotel
4. The Bull Hotel
5. The Swan Hotel
6. The Crown Hotel
7. The Lifeboat Inn
8. The Bell Hotel
9. The Scole Inn
10. The Old Ferry Boat Inn
11. The Golden Lion Hotel

THE RED LION HOTEL
The hidden room where evil resided

THE RED LION HOTEL ⬛✕
43 HIGH STREET
COLCHESTER, ESSEX
TEL: 01206 577986

Colchester is Britain's oldest recorded town and was its first Roman capital. The tide of history has swept over its ancient streets, and ghosts galore reside within its picturesque buildings. One of the most attractive is The Red Lion Hotel, one of East Anglia's oldest inns, whose timbered frontage has looked down on the High Street since 1465. It was originally built as a private residence for the Howard family, whose coat of arms displayed the white lion (believed to have been the original name of the hostelry). By 1633 the name had changed to The Red Lion, at which time the old building may well have acquired its resident revenant. For this was the year that a lady named Alice Miller was 'foully done to death' here, an event that so peeved her spirit that it has remained at the inn ever since to chill the blood and tingle the spines of all who chance upon her.

Chambermaids working in the bedrooms have heard their names being whispered behind them. Turning to see who is calling them, they always find that there is no one there. Staff have often felt the unnerving sensation that they are being watched, although by whom is anyone's guess. During redevelopment at the hotel in 1972, builders uncovered a walled-off section that had evidently once been part of a room. There was much speculation that they had stumbled upon the inn's legendary 'haunted room', a place possessed of such a fearful reputation in the past that staff were banned from discussing it for fear they would frighten the guests. There were rumours that something terrible had happened in the room long ago, but whether or not the event was related to the murder of Alice Miller is debatable. What is certain, however, was that whenever guests came to hear of the room's reputation, they would take fright and leave immediately.

Eventually trade was so badly affected that the building's older portion was closed down and the haunted room sealed up. The old room remained hidden away and cobwebbed until its rediscovery in 1972, by which time memories of its ghostly past were long forgotten. But the reopening of the room did not reawaken whatever malevolent force once resided therein, for it is now generally agreed that, although there are ghosts at The Red Lion, they are on the whole friendly and harmless.

Opposite: The Scole Inn in Diss has more than its fair share of odd occurrences.

THE THORN HOTEL
The Witch-finder General

THE THORN HOTEL 🛏️✕
HIGH STREET
MISTLEY, ESSEX
TEL: 01206 392821

Matthew Hopkins, the self-styled Witch-finder General, was responsible for the deaths of hundreds of unfortunate women during the mania that gripped East Anglia between 1644 and 1646. His victims were deprived of sleep, starved and tortured in order to get them to confess to all manner of heinous, though unlikely, crimes. He used several Essex inns to meet with informers and interrogate his victims, one of which was Mistley's ancient coaching inn, The Thorn.

Staff working in the cellars, where Hopkins is said to have imprisoned his victims, often complain of being overcome by a feeling of desolation and hopelessness. An upstairs room, which he used for his interrogations, is said to possess a more substantial imprint of his reign of terror, and guests have complained of being woken in the night by a strange presence. Meanwhile, the unmistakable figure of Hopkins has been seen sitting in a chair in the attic.

Equally mysterious is the childish shade that has been seen around the premises, thought to be the ghost of a young boy who was play-fighting with a friend in the stables one long ago day, when he accidentally fell beneath a horse and was trampled to death.

THE CROSS KEYS HOTEL
Have yourself a ghostly little Christmas

THE CROSS KEYS HOTEL 🛏️✕
32 HIGH STREET
SAFFRON WALDEN, ESSEX
TEL: 01799 522207

The handsomely timbered Cross Keys Hotel once echoed to the revelries of Parliamentarian soldiers raising their tankards and toasting Oliver Cromwell's victory over Charles I. In those days it was known as The Whalebone, a name it kept until the mid 18th century when it acquired its current appellation.

Haunting at The Cross Keys might not be a regular occurrence throughout the year, but it is most certainly a punctual one. It occurs between 11 p.m. and midnight on Christmas Eve, when slow, ponderous footsteps are heard plodding their way along an upstairs corridor, stopping at the solid wall at the end of the hallway. Although no footsteps are ever heard returning along the corridor, witnesses who rush upstairs to investigate never find a trace of anyone or anything that could have been responsible for the phenomenon. It is believed that the footsteps are those of a ghostly Parliamentarian who was assigned the unenviable task of guarding vanquished Royalists kept as prisoners at the inn in the aftermath of the English Civil War.

THE BULL HOTEL
The phantom whom dogs fear

The Bull looks every inch the traditional English inn. Its splendid timber-framed façade dates back to 1450, when the property was built as a wool merchant's mansion. It became an inn in the 16th century, and in 1648 one Roger Greene

> THE BULL HOTEL 🛏 ✗
> HALL STREET, LONG MELFORD
> SUDBURY, SUFFOLK
> TEL: 01787 378494

stabbed a yeoman farmer by the name of Richard Everard to death in its hallway. According to tradition, the dead man's body was laid out overnight in the hotel's lounge, but by the next morning it had mysteriously vanished. His ghost, however, has been very much in evidence ever since. Many is the time that the heavy oak door leading from the hall to the dining room has been seen to open and close of its own accord.

During the 1970s, The Bull was plagued by poltergeist activity, and objects would be hurled across the dining room by some unseen entity. Chairs would move around overnight, and footsteps were often heard making their way along hotel corridors. Colonel Dawson, the proprietor at this time, decided to investigate one night and took his dog with him. Little good it did him! Once the animal reached the corridor it was struck rigid with terror and crouched in the corner, whimpering. In recent years, however, the revenant of Richard Everard (if he is responsible for the ghostly goings-on) has become somewhat subdued, and supernatural happenings at The Bull have become less common.

THE SWAN HOTEL
The ghostly tickler

Lavenham is one of the most beautiful towns in Britain, and is widely regarded as one of the finest examples of a medieval municipality. The Swan Hotel, parts of which date back to 1425, is without doubt one of Lavenham's chief glories. It is an archetypal medieval inn,

> THE SWAN HOTEL 🛏 ✗
> HIGH STREET
> LAVENHAM, SUFFOLK
> TEL: 01787 247477

with a timbered exterior and beamed ceilings and ancient walls reminiscent of

a bygone age. During World War II its Garden Bar was a great favourite with American airmen stationed nearby, and many of their signatures are scrawled across the walls of the bar. Glenn Miller, the bandleader, is even said to have stopped in for a drink before setting out on his last fateful flight.

However, the building's benign ghost dates back to the 19th century when The Swan was in its heyday as a coaching inn. What is now room 15 was, in those days, occupied by a housekeeper. It is said that she fell pregnant out of wedlock, and although the man responsible agreed to marry her, he had a last-minute change of heart and left her standing at the altar. Another version of the tale claims that she became depressed when she was overlooked for a promotion. Whatever the cause, the outcome was the same: the poor woman hanged herself from one of the rafters in her room. Her ghost has remained behind to chill the blood of those who cross her path. A security guard encountered her in 1991 and was scared half out of his wits. And a nun who stayed in room 15 awoke with a start in the early hours when the ghost began tickling her feet!

THE CROWN HOTEL
A haunting we will go

The timeless aura that descends upon you as you enter this 15th-century inn, with its inglenook fireplace and low beams, is quaintly reminiscent of a bygone and long lost age. Sitting in its snug and atmospheric bar, listening to

THE CROWN HOTEL
104 HIGH STREET, BILDESTON
IPSWICH, SUFFOLK
TEL: 01449 740510

the low murmur of conversation, it is easy to close your eyes and cast your imagination back over the thousands of events to which its ancient walls must have borne witness.

There was the infamous election campaign of 1855, when The Crown was being used as a political headquarters by one of the candidates and rival supporters attacked it. They shattered the windows, smashed crockery and broke many of the drinking vessels until, their frustrations vented, they proceeded with a noble attempt to drink the pub dry!

Cast your mind further back in time to 1495, and you can imagine the excited chatter as the wool merchant's family, for whom the property was

Opposite: A former smugglers' haunt, The Lifeboat Inn in Thornham is a cosy refuge on a winter's evening. Just beware the ghostly figure with a cape and cutlass.

first built, moved into their brand new home. On opening your eyes, you may just catch a fleeting glimpse of one of the many ghosts that flit about its rooms.

A mysterious grey lady has been seen at a window overlooking the car park, waving a ghostly farewell to departing customers. In other ghost sightings, two children dressed in Victorian outfits have appeared before startled guests at various points around the inn, while an old man in a tri-cornered hat is frequently seen sitting in a favourite corner of the main bar, quietly observing all that goes on.

For those who enjoy a smattering of haunted hospitality, room 4 is the bedroom where guests often experience things going bump in the dead of night. They may be treated to an appearance of the grey lady, or of the 'genial missionary' whose presence several visiting mediums have detected. If neither of these is sufficient to aid a decent night's unrest, there is always the touch of ice-cold fingers that have been known to stroke the necks of sleeping guests.

THE LIFEBOAT INN
The invented ghost that became real

THE LIFEBOAT INN 🛏️ ✗
SHIP LANE
THORNHAM, NORFOLK
TEL: 01485 512236

The 16th-century Lifeboat Inn is as inviting a hostelry as you could wish to stumble upon. It is just the sort of place to pitch up at on one of those cold winter days when a keen breeze drives across the neighbouring sea flats. Log fires blaze in its ancient hearths and oil lamps dangle from its timber ceilings. The walls of its tangled maze of snug rooms are hung with murderous-looking muskets, swords and other paraphernalia, recalling the days when this old hostelry was a notorious smugglers' haunt.

When Angie Coker took over the inn in the late 1990s she decided that all that was missing was a resident ghost. So, when composing the section of the brochure that deals with the wonderfully atmospheric Smugglers' Bar, she wrote that 'should the oak door creak open and a tall dark stranger arrive with a cape and cutlass, it would hardly be a surprise'.

It certainly did, however, come as a surprise to several members of staff who have since caught fleeting glimpses of just such a 'tall, dark stranger' walking across the Smugglers' Bar.

Is it possible that the ambience of the inn being so conducive to things going bump in the night (or day), coupled with Angie's evocative description, has simply evoked autosuggestion in several members of staff? Or could it be that the ghost has been lying dormant for years and Angie's musings have stirred him into at last earning his ghostly keep?

THE BELL HOTEL
Nine ghostly hostess

This 15th-century timbered inn sits peaceably in the centre of Thetford and affords fine views over the River Ouse. Over the centuries it has seen many a proprietor come and go, several of whom have left their mark on the

| THE BELL HOTEL 🛏 🍴 |
| KING STREET |
| THETFORD, NORFOLK |
| TEL: 01842 754455 |

ancient building in one form or another. One tenant, however, has made a more lasting impression and still returns here from time to time to wander through the inn's rooms and corridors.

Betty Radcliffe kept The Bell in the opening years of the 19th century. Recalling her tenure in the mid 1800s, Lord Albermarle wrote of how he used to 'sit down to a most sumptuous breakfast [here] and all for love, and not for money. I was a prime favourite with the landlady ... so much so that for the many years that, as man and boy, I frequented her hostelry, she would never expect a sixpence from me.'

Betty was described as wearing a high cap with a flaxen wig 'which she appeared to have outgrown, for it ill-concealed her grey hairs'. She was a formidable hostess who, 'being the sole proprietress of post-horses into Norfolk ... assumed an independent demeanour and language, to which everyone was compelled to submit'. She had no respect for rank or nobility, and airs and graces cut little ice with her. On one occasion the Duke of York, a regular visitor, is said to have handed her a pile of coins in payment for a change of horses. 'I may as well take a little of your money,' she told him with a grim satisfaction, 'for I have been paying your father's [the King's] taxes for many a long day.'

Betty may have departed physically from The Bell long ago, but her guiding spirit has remained behind to ensure that her inn is run with the smooth efficiency that her customers had come to expect. Several guests have encountered her restless wraith drifting silently along corridors at dead of night. She goes about her ghostly business seemingly oblivious to the bemusement she causes those who encounter her. Considering members of the royal family held no fear for her in life, mere mortals enjoying the hospitality of her lovely old inn today can hold little dread for her in death.

THE SCOLE INN
She never betrayed him

THE SCOLE INN 🛏 🍴
IPSWICH ROAD, SCOLE
DISS, NORFOLK
TEL: 01379 740481

On all counts, The Scole Inn is a striking, imposing and very impressive building. It was built in 1655, has inglenook fireplaces, heavy oak beams and doors, boasts a magnificent carved staircase, and is the haunt of a ghostly lady of mischievous intent.

Nobody knows for certain who the lady was in life, but there is a long-held tradition that in the hotel's distant past her husband became suspicious that she was having an affair. What evidence he had is now long forgotten, but it is generally agreed that his hurt turned to anger and, in a fit of jealous rage, he murdered the poor woman. Presumably his crime was perpetrated in room 2, for that is where the sad shade of a pale lady has been seen on several occasions. Guests have also sensed a presence in this particular room, as if an invisible entity has passed through and left a cold chill in its wake. Some people have even suffered the indignity of having the bed covers tugged off them in the night by an unseen hand, as the ghostly lady continues to remonstrate against the injustice that has left her spirit stranded at the place of her tragic demise.

THE OLD FERRY BOAT INN
Buried beneath the floor

THE OLD FERRY BOAT INN 🍴
NR HOLYWELL, ST IVES
CAMBRIDGESHIRE
TEL: 01480 463227

An isolated setting on the leafy banks of the Great Ouse, a thatched roof over ancient oak beams, beneath which massive inglenook fireplaces blaze a warm welcome, all help make The Old Ferry Boat one of Cambridgeshire's most atmospheric inns. Its stone floor now lies hidden beneath a plush carpet. Except, that is, one rectangular slab of ancient granite which they would never dare cover, for beneath it are said to rest the mortal remains of Juliet Tewslie.

Neglected by her lover, Tom, the inconsolable girl is said to have hanged herself on 17 March in about the year 1078. On finding her body, Tom was overcome with grief and remorse. He cut her down, cradled her lifeless form in his arms and, having bade her a sorrowful farewell, buried her where she had died, marking the grave with the block of granite over which The Old Ferry Boat Inn was later built.

The evening of 17 March is something of a party night at the inn, when the first chimes of midnight are said to bring Juliet Tewslie rising from her grave to float around the pub. Such is her posthumous fame that her appearance is awaited eagerly by locals, international ghost-hunters and the just plain curious, who come to greet the poor girl whose tragic demise, and subsequent nocturnal jaunts, have helped make her one of Cambridgeshire's most abiding annual fixtures.

THE GOLDEN LION HOTEL
The watching eyes of the Green Lady

In the market place of St Ives there stands a statue of Oliver Cromwell. He was born in nearby Huntingdon and, when the statue was cast in the early years of the 20th century, it was intended that it should stand in the

| THE GOLDEN LION HOTEL |
| MARKET HILL |
| ST IVES, CAMBRIDGESHIRE |
| TEL: 01480 492100 |

town of his birth. The good citizens of Huntingdon, however, refused to accept the statue, hence its current location.

Standing across from the statue is The Golden Lion Hotel, a 16th-century coaching inn that has Cromwellian associations in so far as he is once reputed to have stayed here and his ghost is said to return on the 13th day of each month, although no one knows why he should favour this particular date.

The Golden Lion's main phantom is the Green Lady, whom tradition claims may have been Cromwell's mistress. She has a fondness for room 14: witnesses have watched as the bedroom door has opened and closed of its own accord, and several guests have had the bedclothes tugged off them. A portrait hanging on the wall in the restaurant is said to be of the Green Lady, and a peculiar aspect of the picture is that the eyes have the unsettling habit of following you as you walk around the room.

HEART OF ENGLAND

HEREFORDSHIRE, WORCESTERSHIRE, WARWICKSHIRE, GLOUCESTERSHIRE & OXFORDSHIRE

The Shaven Crown Hotel, Shipton-under-Wychwood, Oxfordshire – see page 87
*Brother Sebastian appears to Robert Burpitt in the courtyard
of the Shaven Crown.*

The peaceful countryside that sweeps from the border with Wales to the west and rolls towards London in the east has many a chilling tale. This varied landscape was host to several skirmishes during the Wars of the Roses and the English Civil War, and both have left their mark on the countryside. Several of the inns here acquired their spectres from nearby battles. The delightfully eccentric Castle Inn, for example, stands on the striking summit of Edgehill, where the first major clash between Charles I and the Parliamentarians took place in 1642. The very air around the inn often resounds to the ghostly cries of the dead and dying, while several witnesses have been treated to a grandstand seat as spectral armies re-enact the conflict! But pride of place must go to The Ancient Ram at Wotton-under-Edge. Although it hasn't been an inn since the 1960s, I just had to include it; I don't scare easily, but The Ancient Ram affected me deeply.

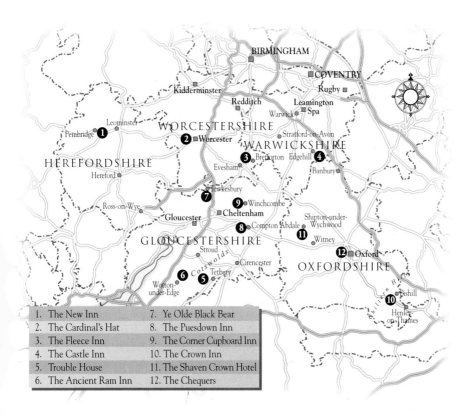

1. The New Inn	7. Ye Olde Black Bear
2. The Cardinal's Hat	8. The Puesdown Inn
3. The Fleece Inn	9. The Corner Cupboard Inn
4. The Castle Inn	10. The Crown Inn
5. Trouble House	11. The Shaven Crown Hotel
6. The Ancient Ram Inn	12. The Chequers

THE NEW INN
If only they could meet

THE NEW INN
MARKET SQUARE, PEMBRIDGE
LEOMINSTER, HEREFORDSHIRE
TEL: 01544 388427

With a striking black-and-white timbered exterior, and an interior resplendent with flagstone floors, oak doors with peg latches, The New Inn boasts an impressive pedigree stretching back almost 700 years. It started out as a farmhouse in 1311, which gives it the impressive distinction of being the oldest New Inn in England. The farmer's wife brewed and sold ale to the merchants at the nearby open market; thus beginning a tradition for hospitality that saw it evolve into a coaching inn that eventually doubled as a courthouse and a prison. Tradition holds that the 1461 treaty, by which Edward IV ascended the throne of England during the Wars of the Roses, was ratified in the courtroom here.

Naturally, The New Inn is haunted, and it is generally agreed that it is inhabited by two ghosts. One is a young woman who awaits the return of her lover from some long-ago war. Nobody knows for certain which war, and whether he was killed or simply deserted her is up for debate. Interestingly, her mournful wraith appears to have had her fill of the fickle nature of the male of the species, since she only ever appears to other women.

Unrelated, though intriguingly coincidental, is the fact that the other spirit is that of a soldier who paces the corridors resplendent in a scarlet tunic, sometimes carrying a sword and at other times beating a drum.

It is not known whether the two phantoms are aware of each other. One can only hope that the day (or night) will come when their spectral paths will cross, and the roving revenants of the old New Inn will be joined together forever in ghostly union!

THE CARDINAL'S HAT
Lederhosen, fire and Emilie's phantom realm

THE CARDINAL'S HAT
31 FRIAR STREET
WORCESTER, WORCESTERSHIRE
TEL: 01905 22066

Between 1100 and 1540 Worcester Cathedral was one of England's principle places of pilgrimage, and numerous ecclesiastical inns were established to provide shelter for travellers. One of the few to survive is The Cardinal's Hat, which has the distinction of being the oldest inn in

Worcester. The first reference to it was in 1497 when it became one of the depots for the city's fire hooks. Fire was a constant threat to the thatched buildings of medieval England, and long hooks, used to tear down the burning thatch, were kept at 'hook houses'. Over the centuries that followed, the inn changed its name several times, becoming The Swan and Falcon in the 18th century, then The Coventry Arms in 1814, as the owner attempted to ingratiate himself with the Earl of Coventry, then Recorder of Worcester.

The inn didn't actually revert to its original name until the 1950s, and it was at this time that rumours of ghostly goings on began to circulate. In a nice reversal of the norm, the temperature in a front second-floor bedroom often increased whenever supernatural phenomena occurred. One landlord recalled how he had been unpacking some boxes in the room when suddenly it became steaming hot. He went out into the corridor but found that the temperature there was normal; on re-entering the bedroom he found it had returned to normal there too. Many people before and since have experienced similar phenomena around that room. Witnesses have spoken of seeing a girl, wearing a white nightdress and with long blonde hair, drifting along the corridor outside. Tradition maintains that she is the ghost of a young woman – possibly an innkeeper's daughter – who died in a fire in the room in the early years of the 20th century.

In 2002, charismatic Austrians Anton Limlei and Andrea Schutz bought the pub and transformed it into an authentic Austrian bar and restaurant. Today lederhosen and dirndl dresses are the order of the day, while the beer, wine and food are specially imported from their homeland. They have grown used to their ghost – whom they have no doubt is benign – and have named her Emilie. Although they have never seen her, they have experienced the occasional spectral prank, such as items being moved around or even disappearing. But a shout of 'Stop it, Emilie' is enough to ensure that order is quickly restored.

THE FLEECE INN
Witches unwelcome

This delightful, timber-framed hostelry was originally a medieval farmhouse, and remained as such until the Taplin family applied for an innkeeper's licence in 1848. It has changed little since, due largely to the fact that it

THE FLEECE INN ✕
THE CROSS, BRETFORTON
EVESHAM, WORCESTERSHIRE
TEL: 01386 831173

stayed in the same family until the death of Lola Taplin in 1977.

On the hearths by the two fireplaces you can still see several curious circles, known as 'witch-marks', dating back to a more superstitious age when it was believed that the sinister sisterhood entered houses via the chimney. Each night, before retiring to bed, successive householders would draw three chalk circles upon the hearth; it was believed that a witch descending the chimney would be trapped inside them until morning, when the daylight would weaken her powers and she would flee. The marks have been drawn so often that they have left indentations in the hearthstones.

It is widely held that the ghost of Lola Taplin haunts The Fleece Inn. This formidable lady ran the pub alone for the last 30 years of her life and was fond of informing customers that they were honoured to be drinking in her home. She always insisted that guests partook only of alcoholic beverages, and food was banned. The rule was relaxed shortly after her death, and Lola appears to have shown her objections in a very direct manner. One customer had placed his sandwich box on one of the tables, when it was suddenly lifted into the air by an invisible hand and flung to the floor, scattering the contents everywhere. On other occasions, ghostly footsteps have been heard around the property, while an unseen force has been known to hurl small objects in what appears to be a phantom fit of pique.

THE CASTLE INN
The battle that never ends

THE CASTLE INN 🛏 ✕
EDGEHILL, NR BANBURY,
OXFORDSHIRE
TEL: 01295 670255

The magnificent and turreted Castle Inn – also known as The Round Tower, or Radway Tower – dates from the 1740s and is a folly built by the architect Sandersen Miller, who based his design on Guy's Tower at Warwick Castle. Its stands on the site where, on Sunday 23 October 1642, King Charles 1 raised his standard and called his officers around him to prepare for the first major battle of the English Civil War. Miller intended it to be both a memorial to the combatants and, so local gossip maintains, a place where he could come to enjoy secret assignations with his mistress! The tower became an inn in 1822 when one of Miller's descendants sold it to an innkeeper. Although The Castle itself is not particularly haunted, it is surrounded by some of the most ghost-infested countryside in Britain.

The Battle of Edgehill was a bloody skirmish in which a Royalist army, numbering some 13,000 men, clashed with a Parliamentarian force numbering slightly less and commanded by Robert Devereaux, Earl of Essex. The early advantage went to the Royalists, until King Charles's nephew, Prince Rupert of the Rhine, squandered it with an ill-advised cavalry charge that left the infantry exposed to an enemy attack. The Roundheads succeeded in capturing the royal standard and killing its bearer, Sir Edmund Verney. A Royalist cavalry officer, Captain John Smith, spotted a group of enemy troops making off with the colours. He charged after them, retrieved the standard and returned it to the King, with Verney's hand still clasped around it!

Three thousand men lost their lives that October day and, with the outcome of the battle indecisive, both sides were quick to claim the victory. The advantage probably did go to the King's army and, had Charles then chosen to march on London, he may well have altered the course of history. But so appalled was he by the carnage of this battle that he was unable to concentrate on military strategy and opted instead to head for Oxford, where he established his headquarters.

On 23 December 1642, several shepherds at Edgehill claimed to have witnessed a spectral re-enactment of the entire skirmish. It began with the sound of distant drums, which were joined by 'the noise of soldiers ... giving out their last groans'. There then appeared in the air 'the same incorporeall souldiers that made those clamours' and a full-scale clash of phantom armies took place in the sky above the original battlefield. The shepherds rushed to nearby Kineton, where they repeated, on oath, before William Wood – a Justice of the Peace – and the Reverend Samuel Marshall the unbelievable details of what they had witnessed. The phantom armies reappeared over several nights and were witnessed on Christmas Day by many people in 'the same tumultuous and warlike manner ... fighting with as much spite and spleen as formerly'. When word of the miracle reached the King in Oxford, he dispatched six men of 'good repute and integrity' to investigate. They too were treated to a ghostly re-enactment of the dreadful battle and three of them actually recognized several of the ghostly combatants.

In the mid 19th century a group of journalists headed for Edgehill to investigate reports that a spectral army had been seen lined up along the ridge. So unnerved were they by their subsequent experience that 'they all returned shaking and frightened, and went off home as fast as they could'. The hoof beats of invisible cavalryman have been heard thundering down nearby roads in the dead of night, while the agonized screams of the wounded and dying are said to rend the air around

The Castle Inn from time to time. People do claim to catch occasional glimpses of ethereal soldiers in the pub's bar – the walls of which are adorned with muskets, halberds and breastplates – but these sightings pale into insignificance when compared to the plethora of phantoms swirling across the landscape around what is, without doubt, one of England's most unusual inns.

TROUBLE HOUSE
Trouble at the bar

TROUBLE HOUSE ✗
CIRENCESTER, TETBURY
GLOUCESTERSHIRE
TEL: 01666 502206

The fickle finger of fate appears to have pointed a bony digit at former proprietors of this hostelry with an alarming regularity. It has catered to the needs of hungry and thirsty travellers for over 300 years and was once called The Waggon and Horses. Tetbury carpenter John Reeve built the inn in 1755. Two years later John Bird took on the lease, and the first hint of tragedy struck when several of his wives died young. By the 1770s the inn was being leased by Richard Reeve, son of its builder, who hit a sticky financial patch when many of his male customers were forcibly abducted by His Majesty's press gangs to fight in the American Revolution.

The inn was caught up in the 1830 agricultural riots as local labourers vented their displeasure at the introduction of mechanical haymaking and threshing machines. One day a wagon was passing through Tetbury, supposedly laden with hay, when someone happened to notice a haymaking machine hidden among the stack. An angry mob gave chase and, having surrounded the wagon outside the pub, set fire to it. Unfortunately the flames spread to the inn's thatched roof, causing severe damage. It was subsequently restored and a tiled roof added.

The pub's financial fortunes then suffered a severe downturn. Tradition holds that a landlord, who had sunk every last penny into it, went bankrupt and hanged himself from a beam inside the inn. His successor fared little better and drowned himself in a nearby pond.

By the early 1900s, it was well known that the ghosts of the two landlords roamed the premises, and the inn's stormy past led to its being

Opposite: The Ancient Ram Inn appears to have sunk into the ground. Maybe the weight of the evil forces at work within its ancient walls are responsible?

renamed 'Trouble House'. Surprisingly, however, there was no shortage of landlords willing to take the risk and tackle whatever malevolent force might be lurking within. As the 20th century progressed, the fortunes of the old inn drifted into calmer times; the ghostly suicides gradually faded away, and are now little more than distant memories.

THE ANCIENT RAM INN
Ghosts in every nook and cranny

THE ANCIENT RAM INN
WOTTON-UNDER-EDGE, GLOUCESTERSHIRE
TEL: 01453 842598

The Ancient Ram Inn possesses a genuinely chilling aura, and a reputation that is so menacing that many local people won't even walk past it at night. The building is thought to date from around 1145, and it has been suggested that the workmen who built the parish church opposite were lodged here. It served for a time as a priest's house before converting to an inn. Its last pint was pulled in 1968. Once it had closed for business John Humphries, who is now the sole permanent living occupant, purchased the building from the brewery. He has been battling to save the structure ever since, irrespective of the endeavours by former residents to interfere as much as possible.

The moment you enter the old inn, an aura of dreadful foreboding envelopes you. The bare walls, creaking floorboards, steep stairs and mysterious shadows are sufficient to elicit the coldest of shivers; while the legions of ghost stories that come marching from its mist-shrouded past can chill the blood of even the most steadfast cynic.

'The atmosphere was awful,' is how one visitor put it, 'I can only describe it as pure filth – dark and heavy.'

The first room that visitors encounter is the 'Men's Kitchen'. This reputedly stands on the site of a pagan burial ground, and the disturbing sound of a baby crying is often heard here. People ascending the steep staircase up to the first floor have been thrown up the stairs by invisible hands. A photograph taken here in June 1999 showed a mysterious white mist, about the height of a human, ascending the staircase.

On the first floor is The Ram's most haunted and terrifying room, the Bishop's Room. A medium pushing open its door was once lifted off the ground and flung across the corridor. The atmosphere inside is oppressive and disturbing. A ghostly cavalier has been known to materialize by the dressing table and stride purposefully across to the opposite wall. Two monks have been seen shimmering in one corner. Witnesses have heard the terrified screams of a man who was, reputedly, murdered here by having his head thrust into the fire. A phantom shepherd and his dog have been seen near the door, while those who spend the night in the room have often attracted the lustful attentions of either an incubus or a succubus.

'Rather a lot for one room,' observed John Humphries to me with decided understatement.

Climbing into the attic and crouching beneath the roof timbers, a feeling of intense melancholy appears to hang in the air. An innkeeper's daughter is said to have been murdered in this roof space in the early 1500s, and people attempting to sleep in the Bishop's Room below often hear the sound of 'something heavy' being dragged across the floor above their heads.

There is little doubt that the spirits and demons that reside within the walls of The Ancient Ram Inn are extremely active. It is a place where nightmares abound, and is certainly not for those of a nervous disposition. But to cross its threshold is to step back in time, and the chance of an encounter with one of its many ghosts is not to be missed.

YE OLDE BLACK BEAR

The headless man with the clanking chains

Dating back to 1309 and occupying a riverside location, The Olde Black Bear has the distinction of being the oldest inn in Gloucestershire. It is a wonderful place of beamed, panelled corridors and creaking floors, across

| YE OLDE BLACK BEAR ✖ |
| 68 HIGH STREET |
| TEWKESBURY, GLOUCESTERSHIRE |
| TEL: 01684 292202 |

which a headless figure has been known to stroll, dragging his chains behind him in true ghostly fashion!

The ghost's deficiency in the head department has made identification impossible, but since his fashion sense appears to be that of the 14th century, it has been suggested that he might be the one of the Lancastrians whose army was defeated by the Yorkists at the Battle of Tewkesbury in 1471. Many of the vanquished soldiers headed for Tewkesbury, and a fair number of them sought shelter at The Olde Black Bear.

Perhaps he is the shade of one of their number who was decapitated in the heat of battle and who, not realizing he was dead, followed his comrades as they fled the field, and pitched up at this ancient place where he has remained ever since.

THE PUESDOWN INN
The ghostly highwayman and the phantom coach

The Puesdown Inn's origins are said to stretch back to 1236, and for most of its working life it has operated as a coaching inn. Its remote location (it stands today on the A40's highest point) also made it a favoured haunt of highwaymen.

THE PUESDOWN INN 🛏 ✗
COMPTON ABDALE, CHELTENHAM
GLOUCESTERSHIRE
TEL: 01451 860262

The inn's most persistent spectral visitor is said to be one of these 'gentlemen of the road' who, having being shot in the course of his nefarious business, staggered back to the inn, where he banged hard and long upon the door. When the landlord eventually answered, it was too late. The highwayman's lifeless body came crashing towards him, flinging his spirit across the threshold where it has remained in residence ever since.

Ghostly knocking is often heard on the front door. Phantom footsteps heard crossing the lounge, and then ascending the stairs, have often disturbed the peace. One landlord claimed he was woken by strange sounds outside and, climbing out of bed, was astonished to see a ghostly coach pulling into the yard. Other people looking out of their windows at dead of night have spied a dark figure galloping away on a horse. An Australian couple was lying in bed one night when the husband awoke to find that an invisible 'something' was slowly tugging the bedclothes off the bed. And finally, inexplicable wet patches have been known to appear on the upstairs carpet – although whether these are connected to the ghost is unrecorded.

THE CORNER CUPBOARD INN
She wears a blue dress

Although The Corner Cupboard Inn is one of Winchcombe's oldest buildings, it is one of its newest inns, and did not acquire a licence until 1877. It was built as a farmhouse around 1550, using stones from the

THE CORNER CUPBOARD INN ✗
83 GLOUCESTER STREET
WINCHCOMBE, GLOUCESTERSHIRE
TEL: 01242 602303

recently dissolved Winchcombe Abbey. The unusual name of the pub

Opposite: The Crown Inn at Pishill is a charming place to meet friends – and be sure to say hello to the ghost of Father Dominique when you drop by.

came about in the 1940s when a visiting RAF officer was so taken by its maze of corridors and dark corners that he dubbed it the 'Corner Cupboard'.

Legend holds that at some stage in the latter half of the 19th century a young girl who worked at the inn refused to submit to the landlord's lustful advances. So angered was he by her rejection that he threw her to her death down the steps that still exist at the back of the pub. Her ghost, which witnesses describe as being around 12 or 13 years old and wearing a blue dress, has haunted the pub ever since.

The young girl has mostly been sighted towards the back of the restaurant, and glimpses of her tend to be somewhat fleeting. However, staff and customers in the bar have frequently been startled by the sound of child-like footsteps running across the upstairs room, even though it is known to be empty and there are no children on the premises. More unnerving is the rocking chair in this same room that is often heard moving back and forth of its own accord.

Then there was the barmaid who worked at the inn for many years and who liked nothing better than to sit in the bar of an evening with a glass of cider. Usually she would be allowed to enjoy her tipple in peace. But if she ever wore a blue dress, the ghost would respond by lifting the glass and emptying her drink into her lap. Evidently The Corner Cupboard's phantom jealously guards her fashion sense!

THE CROWN INN
The ghostly moonlight sonata

> THE CROWN INN ✗
> PISHILL, HENLEY-ON-THAMES
> OXFORDSHIRE
> TEL: 01491 638364

It has been suggested that in days gone by, when horses would haul huge wagons up the hill that passes The Crown Inn, they would be allowed to stop at the top to relieve themselves. Thus the village acquired its name, which is actually pronounced 'Pizz'l'. That, at least, is the explanation you might hear in The Crown's public bar. In the more refined lounge bar they favour the theory that the name comes from the Anglo-Saxon *Pushill*, 'the hill on which peas grow'.

Whatever the explanation, there can be no disagreement over the fact that The Crown is one of the loveliest inns imaginable. It dates from the 15th century and is one of the oldest properties in the village. It is also haunted, its ghost belonging to the days of the Catholic persecutions in

England when the nearby mansion of Stonor House became a papist stronghold and priests were, reputedly, smuggled here to be hidden in a specially constructed 'priest's hole' in the attic of the inn.

One such priest was Father Dominique, who now haunts the snug interior of The Crown. There are two versions of what happened to him. The first maintains that he either seduced – or was seduced by – one of the pub's serving wenches, and felt so guilty that he hanged himself from a beam. The second follows the first as far as the seduction goes, but then holds that Father Dominique was hiding at the inn when he heard his lover being molested by a drunken customer. Determined to protect her honour, he raced from his hiding place and was promptly killed by her assailant.

His ghostly image, in a black coat and wide-brimmed hat, has been repeatedly seen around the inn. Occasionally the mysterious sound of loud thumping is also heard echoing from the attic. Mediums have detected a 'presence' towards the back of the premises, although they are unable to say for sure whether it is the spirit of the gallant Father Dominique. Equally mysterious was the phantom pianist who used to play the pub's piano at dead of night. Whether or not this was Father Dominique tinkling the ivory in a moonlight sonata to his lady-love is not known. But the night hours are peaceful now, for the landlord was unimpressed by the disturbances, and had the piano removed!

THE SHAVEN CROWN HOTEL
The ghost of Brother Sebastian

Built around 1380, The Shaven Crown was originally a hostelry for the monks of neighbouring Bruern Abbey. But following the monastery's dissolution in 1534, the

THE SHAVEN CROWN HOTEL 🛏 ✗
HIGH STREET
SHIPTON-UNDER-WYCHWOOD, OXFORDSHIRE
TEL: 01993 830330

building lay deserted until Elizabeth I turned it into a hunting lodge. In 1580 the Queen presented the lodge to the village on condition that it became an inn, and thus began a tradition for hospitality that has continued to this day. During World War II it was pressed into the service of the nation and acquired perhaps its most notorious resident, the fascist leader Oswald Mosley, who was incarcerated here for six months.

Today it is a comfortable hotel where guests can experience a delightfully archaic slice of bygone England. Stepping from the outside highway and pushing open the heavy door, you are confronted by a resident's lounge that would not be out of place in a medieval castle. Mellowed walls of solid Cotswold stone soar up to what is, without doubt, The Shaven Crown's chief glory: its double-collar braced roof. It stands as a proud testimony to the skills of the ecclesiastical craftsmen who constructed it over 600 years ago. Its rafters must have witnessed the comings and goings of tens of thousands of people, one of whom – a phantom monk known as Brother Sebastian – still makes occasional ghostly forays to the place for which he, evidently, held great affection in life.

Brother Sebastian is a harmless old fellow who seems to have a particular fondness for room 11, where his spirit has been encountered at all hours of the day and night. A chef once saw him emerge from the room, cross the corridor and melt into a wall opposite. A cleaner who has worked at the hotel for 40 years sees him quite regularly and, although acknowledging that he is not in the least bit frightening, she always insists that the door be left open when she is working in room 11.

Robert Burpitt, who with his wife, Jane, owns and runs The Shaven Crown, was crossing the courtyard one night when he heard the distinctive sound of plainsong drifting upon the breeze. Suddenly a faint light appeared before him, and there stood the shimmering shade of Brother Sebastian. Many guests have seen this same figure either ascending the stairs or walking along corridors. But although his sudden appearances can be startling, he is certainly not evil. Indeed, there is no doubt that the overall ambience of this historic old inn is both spiritual and relaxing. And if a long-ago resident wants to keep a watchful eye on the well-being of guests, then Amen to that!

THE CHEQUERS
The tunnelling friars

THE CHEQUERS ✗
HIGH STREET
OXFORD, OXFORDSHIRE
TEL: 01865 726904

The building that is now The Chequers began life as a private house in the latter half of the 13th century. By 1434 it was being used by a moneylender who, in 1460, began conducting his business under the sign of The Chequer. The name remained when, 40 years later, one Richard Kent transformed the building into the rambling tavern that today stands proudly overlooking Oxford's High Street. The oak panelling, plasterwork ceilings, carved stonework and ancient fireplace might seem a little at odds with the inn's bustling vibrancy, but the combination of youthful exuberance and cobwebbed antiquity imbues the place with a genuine, albeit curious, charm.

The pub also boasts a splendid example of an English tavern clock that dates from 1760, and around which a colourful legend has been woven. It is said that whenever the clock is wound up, a ghostly monk will appear. He is, according to tradition, connected with a secret tunnel that once ran between The Chequers and another ancient Oxford inn, The Mitre.

Nobody knows for certain the full story behind the fate that befell him, but it is generally agreed that it happened 'a long time ago'! He and a group of his brethren were up to no good in the underground passage one night, when by some cruel twist of fate – or, in another version, divine intervention – they managed to get trapped inside. Their spirits have remained confined there ever since. Tradition holds that in the early hours of some mornings, as the old timbers settle, the ghostly monks can be heard scratching and moaning, desperately trying to attract attention in the forlorn hope that some kind soul will release them and end their dreadful torment.

THE MIDLANDS
NORTHAMPTONSHIRE, LEICESTERSHIRE, LINCOLNSHIRE, NOTTINGHAMSHIRE & THE WEST MIDLANDS

The Old Red Lion, Litchborough, Towcester, Northamptonshire – see page 92

George Bates dies on his enemy's grave, his tailcoat speared by his own sword.

The counties whose roaming revenants are covered in this chapter are home to some of the best-known legends of English history, and many of the ghosts that haunt the region's inns reflect this past. Mary Queen of Scots is perhaps the most famous, but several lesser-known phantoms make regular returns to places they knew in life. Ghostly monks and centuries-old murder victims are just some of the spectres to be encountered in hostelries that range from simple local pubs and cosy old inns to luxury hotels. Nottingham's Ye Olde Trip to Jerusalem, apparently hewn from the rock on which the town's castle stands, has an ambience unlike any other hostelry in England, and the story of its cursed galleon has intrigued me for many years. The White Hart Hotel in Lincoln is as haunted a hotel as you could ever wish to encounter, while elsewhere you will find taverns with an almost dreamlike quality.

1. The Old Red Lion
2. The Talbot Hotel
3. The Black Lion
4. The Blue Bell
5. The White Hart Hotel
6. The Leagate Inn
7. The Sun Inn
8. The Angel and Royal Hotel
9. Ye Olde Trip to Jerusalem

THE OLD RED LION
Grabbed by the ghoulies

THE OLD RED LION ✗
BANBURY ROAD, LITCHBOROUGH
TOWCESTER, NORTHAMPTONSHIRE
TEL: 01327 830250

The Old Red Lion stands opposite the parish church of St Martin's, a proximity that in the 19th century led to a tragedy that, although strictly speaking not a ghost story, should act as a salutary tale to anyone who might be tempted to speak ill of the dead.

One night a group of pub regulars was happily quaffing away when their conversation turned to 'Old Albert', a villager who had recently died and had that day been buried in the churchyard. The general consensus was that the old boy had been a pillar of the community and would be sorely missed. Suddenly one of their number – an irascible character by the name of George Bates – leapt to his feet and, in a drunken diatribe, accused his companions of gross hypocrisy. Albert, he slurred, had been a miserable good-for-nothing, and the village was better off without him. His fellow drinkers warned him not to be so uncharitable, but George wasn't listening. It was then that Nobby Clark suggested that if George hated Albert so much he should show his disdain by taking a sword that hung above the fireplace, cross the road to the churchyard and plunge it into the old man's grave. Without a second thought, George snatched the sword, headed out into the night and that was the last time he was seen alive.

Early next morning the local gravedigger arrived at the churchyard to prepare for a burial. He discovered George's body lying across Albert's grave, his face contorted in terror. His hands were frozen around the old sword, which had been plunged through his tailcoat and into the soil. A doctor was called; after a brief examination he pronounced that George Bates had died of a heart attack, apparently brought on by fright.

It was only when his fellow drinkers came forward a few days later to tell of his last drunken night that the events leading up to his death could be pieced together. Evidently he had marched into the churchyard and attempted to plunge the sword into the mound. But he was so intoxicated that he inadvertently speared his tailcoat, lost his balance and fell across the grave. He attempted to get to his feet, but the sword held him fast. Had he then believed that old Albert had reached from the grave and taken hold of him as

Opposite: The staircase at Oundle's Talbot Hotel came from nearby Fotheringay Castle and with it came the shade of one of England's busiest ghosts, Mary Queen of Scots.

punishment for the desecration? Had he struggled long and hard until his terror brought on the heart attack that killed him? That's certainly what they believed in the taproom of the Old Red Lion, and for years afterwards they would remember the foolish man who in daring to speak ill of the dead had, in a glorious twist of irony, meted out a terrible retribution upon himself.

THE TALBOT HOTEL
Mary Queen of Scots on the old staircase

THE TALBOT HOTEL 🛏 ✗
NEW STREET
OUNDLE, NORTHAMPTONSHIRE
TEL: 01832 273621

With the possible exception of Anne Boleyn, Mary Queen of Scots must have possessed one of the most psychically charged personas ever to drift across the pages of history. There is hardly a castle or house that she visited – and several that she didn't – which is not now haunted by her tragic shade. You would certainly expect to encounter her wraith at Fotheringay Castle, in the great hall of which she was beheaded on 8 February 1587. But the castle was demolished long ago and all that now remains is a melancholic mound in the grounds of a farmhouse. Much of its stone was used for new building in the neighbourhood and many of its furnishings ended up at sundry other locations.

When Mary's son James I ordered that Fotheringay Castle was to be razed to the ground, the landlord of The Talbot Inn, William Whitwell, saw an opportunity to refurbish his hostelry in grand style at reasonable cost and purchased many of the fixtures and fittings. Since the inn was reputedly founded in AD638, it was no doubt in need of a little modernization, and the great horn windows from Fotheringay must have looked particularly impressive when they had been incorporated into its ancient walls. Whitwell also purchased the staircase down which the Queen had walked to her execution and with it, at no extra cost, came Mary's ghost.

On the polished wood of the balustrade can still be seen the imprint of a crown, which local tradition maintains was left by the ring on Mary's finger as she supported herself on her way to the block. Less obtrusive is the psychic imprint of her restless wraith that has been encountered by many of the guests who come to enjoy the traditional hospitality offered by this venerable old establishment. People complain of a feeling of chilling unease as they descend the stairs.

One woman, lying in bed one night, suddenly felt a weight pressing upon the covers. Reaching for the light switch she found herself unable to move as a clammy presence held her firmly against the bed. An invisible hand sometimes moves furniture about, and the picture that depicts Mary's execution has been known suddenly to jump off the wall. Guests crossing the outside yard have seen the ghostly face of a woman staring down from the horn windows that came from Fotheringay. Claims that it is Mary Queen of Scots who haunts The Talbot are little more than convenient speculation, and some even cast doubt on the authenticity of the staircase.

There is, however, a direct physical connection between the tragic Queen and the ancient hostelry. Her executioner lodged at The Talbot Inn the night before she was beheaded where, it is recorded, he 'partook of pigeon pie, drank a quart of best ale and made a merry discourse with the serving girl till an early hour of the morning'.

THE BLACK LION
A ghostly man and his phantom dog

It is said that in the late 19th century that, having killed his mistress, Annie Pritchard, Andrew McRae boiled her head in the huge copper that he kept at The Black Lion, and which was

THE BLACK LION ✕
1 BLACK LION HILL
NORTHAMPTON, NORTHAMPTONSHIRE
TEL: 01604 639472

normally used to prepare the bacon that he sold at Northampton market. His crime was discovered and he was sentenced to death on Christmas Eve 1892. On the night of the murder their baby had also disappeared and was never seen again.

This tragic event may lie behind the infantile sobs that have been known to disturb the peace of the early hours at The Black Lion. The cellars are thought to be the epicentre of the pub's hauntings, and animals show a marked reluctance to enter them. Landlords have witnessed a hazy vapour in the cellar that drifts slowly past them, leaving an icy chill in its wake. A team of ghost-hunters that spent several nights in the cellar was rewarded by the appearance of a flickering light that danced before them, while several claimed to have seen a mysterious figure moving about in the shadows.

However, the most significant event at this haunted hostelry afflicted former landlord Timothy Webb, who was in his bedroom one night when a heavy-set man with a large black dog suddenly appeared before him. Mistaking him for an intruder, he told him in no uncertain terms to get out, whereupon both figures simply vanished into thin air!

THE BLUE BELL
The haunted well

THE BLUE BELL ✗
SHEPHERD'S WALK, BELMESTHORPE
STAMFORD, LINCOLNSHIRE
TEL: 01780 763859

This delightful inn is the haunt of a mysterious figure that has a chilling habit of disappearing when looked at or spoken to. His comings and goings may be linked to the fact that two wells are situated on either side of the bar. Although they have long been sealed up, no one appears to have told the ghost, for tradition holds that he roams the pub on an eternal quest to fetch water. Some witnesses say that he resembles a monk, while others claim that his garb is more that of a member of the laity. However, there is common consensus that his figure is stooped, on account of his having a hunchback. His favoured time to manifest is as closing time approaches, when a sudden and alarming drop in temperature often presages his appearances. Those who experience it will be overcome by a feeling that something strange is standing behind them and, on turning round, will see his spectral figure shuffling towards one of the wells. But should they look at him too closely or, even worse, speak to him, the phantom appears to take umbrage, fixes them with a reproachful glare, and suddenly dissolves in front of them.

THE WHITE HART HOTEL
Lincoln's most haunted building

THE WHITE HART HOTEL 🛏✗
BAILGATE, LINCOLN
TEL: 01522 526222

Nestling within the majestic shadow of Lincoln Cathedral, The White Hart is a veritable time capsule. Its exact age is uncertain, but it was certainly well established by 1387 in which year King Richard II and his Queen, Anne of Bohemia, came to stay. Richard's symbol was a white hart, and it was in honour of his visit that the inn acquired the name by which it has been known ever since. Over succeeding centuries so many memorable events have left their psychic imprint upon the inn's fabric that the old building now has the enviable reputation of being regarded as Lincoln's most haunted building.

A little girl who wears a mob cap and who was, it is reputed, murdered by the inn's rat-catcher, has often been seen in a corner of the first floor. She cowers against the wall, her eyes wide with fear as her ghost is forced to relive the ordeal of her final moments. Then there is the room where, on a Bank

Holiday Monday in the 1960s, one of the guests put the barrel of a shotgun in his mouth and left both a physical and psychical stain upon the surrounding walls. Some people occupying the room have been moved to comment on its sad aura, while others claim to have heard the disturbing sounds of an unseen man weeping.

An equally gruesome, though much older, event lies behind the terrifying spectre that appears beneath the orange dome at the centre of The White Hart. The courtyard and stables were once situated hereabouts, and in the days when the old inn was an important stopover for coaches and travellers bound for York or London it would have been a bustling hub of activity. The country roads at that time were dangerous places, beset by highwaymen and footpads. On one occasion a coachman inflicted horrendous injuries upon one of these 'gentlemen of the road' by thrusting a burning torch into his face as he tried to rob him. The highwayman's ghost is said to roam what was the courtyard, still seeking revenge upon the coachman who maimed him. Guests who have seen his hideous spectre describe him as a 'Don Cortez'-like figure whose face is so obscured by a cloak that only two deep brown eyes can be seen gazing out from the folds of the garment.

The final ghost to wander the ancient hostelry is that of the so-called 'Ginger Jar' man, who haunts one of the suites on the third floor. He cuts quite a dash as he flits hither and thither, dressed in a 1920s caramel-coloured smoking jacket resplendent with an elegant cream cravat. He is believed to have been a former owner of the hotel who occupied the suite of rooms where his nebulous meanderings now occur. Tradition holds the poor old soul was once robbed of his treasured ginger jar, and found its loss such an ordeal that his troubled spirit still wanders the hotel in a desperate search to be reunited with his beloved possession!

THE LEAGATE INN
In from the fens and marshes

The creeper-clad walls of this ancient hostelry blend harmoniously into their surroundings, and no one who ventures to this little corner of rural Lincolnshire can deny that The Leagate Inn exists in a time warp. It was established in 1542

THE LEAGATE INN ⊨ ✗
LEAGATE ROAD
CONINGSBY, LINCOLN
TEL: 01526 342370

and started life as a fen guide house. An iron ring which would once have held a flaming torch to guide night-time travellers across the treacherous fens is still visible on an outside wall. Many a weary wayfarer must have increased their pace on spotting its fiery glow through the bleak mid-winter blizzards, knowing that a warm welcome was waiting.

However, there were others for whom the inn was a less welcoming sight. The enclosure at the front, known as Gibbet Nook Close, was once the site of a gibbet or gallows. It is said that the condemned felons were given the last rites before an engraving of the Last Supper that hangs over the fireplace in the lounge. They were then hanged, and their bodies left swinging in the gibbet as a warning to others who might be contemplating similar transgressions.

One of the unfortunate felons appears to have found the allure of the inn so irresistible that he is loath to move on. Jack Cooper, as regulars know the ghost, favours quiet winter afternoons rather than storm-tossed nights. He appears in the inglenook fireplace attired in the garb of a 16th-century tradesman or artisan. He is, as landlord and landlady Mark and Sharon Dennison so eloquently put it, 'a moving sculpture of a moment in time long ago, there to remind us that we too may become fleeting images to future visitors of the old Leagate'.

THE SUN INN
Murder and a rare stake

THE SUN INN ✗
20 BRIDGE STREET
SAXILBY, LINCOLNSHIRE
TEL: 01522 702326

Tom Otter was a thoroughly dissolute rogue who lodged in an upstairs room of Saxilby's Sun Inn in the early 19th century. He had taken up with a young girl by the name of Mary Kirkham, and by 1805 she was pregnant with his child. In a rare gentlemanly gesture, Tom Otter attempted to make amends for having done the *un*decent thing by doing the decent thing, and on 3 November 1805, despite the hindrance of his already having a wife, he and Mary were married. That night, as they walked home together, Tom Otter reverted to type and murdered his new wife by driving a hedge stake into her heart. Dropping the murder weapon at the scene, he disappeared.

His crime was soon discovered, and Mary's body, along with the stake, was taken back to The Sun Inn. As she was carried up the steps, her blood dripped onto the stones, and despite the efforts of successive landlords to remove them, the stains remained visible for many years.

The stake became a celebrated fixture, and for many years was proudly displayed behind the bar. Legend holds that on the anniversary of the murder it would mysteriously disappear and would always be found next morning at the site of the murder, 'wet with gore'. Eventually the Bishop of Lincoln decided enough was enough. In an attempt to exorcise whatever mischievous spirit was responsible, he burnt the stake in the yard outside the cathedral.

Tom Otter was caught and charged with Mary's murder. His trial took place at The Sun Inn and, having been found guilty, he was sentenced to hang. Following his execution his body was bound in irons and suspended from a high post by way of demonstrating to all who passed by that justice had been done. Unfortunately, such was the weight of the irons that the body twice fell from the post, killing a man on the second occasion.

As a result, The Sun Inn has a few ghost stories to chill the blood of the curious visitor. Tom Otter's wraith is said to roam the premises and is, on occasion, accompanied by a 'female presence' that may, or may not, be Mary Kirkham. Strange noises have been heard at dead of night, and witnesses have felt a cold breeze as though an invisible form has walked past, while a putrid smell has been known to linger in the air. One group of ghost-hunters who joined hands in a circle in an attempt to communicate with the spirits had their wrists gripped by icy fingers and their arms tugged up into the air!

THE ANGEL AND ROYAL HOTEL
The royal prince who was no angel

The Angel and Royal Hotel boasts a spectacular 15th-century façade, resplendent with time-worn grotesques and weather-beaten carvings. An angel holding a crown gazes down from the arch

> THE ANGEL AND ROYAL HOTEL 🛏 ✕
> HIGH STREET
> GRANTHAM, LINCOLNSHIRE
> TEL: 01476 565816

through which coaches once trundled, en route for London, York or Scotland. On either side of the arch are stone depictions of Edward III and Queen Phillipa, commemorating their visit in the 14th century. By that time the Angel Inn, as it was then known, was already approaching old age, having been founded by the Knights Templars over 100 years earlier. King John had lodged there in 1209 and came back again in 1213 during his 'disagreement' with the English barons.

Other monarchs to have graced the old hostelry include Richard III, who occupied the grand state room (now a dining room) in 1483. From here he wrote to the Lord Chancellor requesting that the Great Seal be despatched to him from London so that he might sign the death warrant for the Duke of Buckingham, who was leading a rebellion against him. In 1706 a landlord of The Angel died and left the sum of £2 a year to pay for a sermon to be preached every Christmas, warning the parishioners against the evils of drunkenness. The custom is still observed today.

One person who would certainly have paid little heed to the Christmas sermon was the decidedly libertine Prince of Wales, later Edward VII, who stayed here in 1866. To honour his visit they decided on a slight change of name. The original choice was The Royal Angel, but this was discreetly rejected on the grounds that although the prince was Royal he was certainly no Angel. A compromise was eventually reached, and so the inn became the Angel and Royal.

Today the inn remains much as it would have looked to the thousands of travellers, royal or otherwise, who ducked beneath its timbered ceilings in days of yore. But every so often the old wooden boards on the first and second floors can be heard creaking wearily in the dead of night. Then is the time to snuggle down beneath the blankets. For the sounds mark the passage of the hotel's mysterious white lady who periodically undertakes a phantom stroll along the corridors, intent on some ghostly quest.

YE OLDE TRIP TO JERUSALEM
The cursed galleon

The imposing crag of volcanic rock on which Nottingham Castle stands is honeycombed by a network of caves, several of which are incorporated into what claims to be England's oldest pub, Ye Olde Trip to

YE OLDE TRIP TO JERUSALEM ✗
BREWHOUSE YARD, CASTLE ROAD
NOTTINGHAM, NOTTINGHAMSHIRE
TEL: 0115 947 3171

Jerusalem, established in 1189. A 'trip' in those days was a place to rest and break your journey, and the pub's unusual name derives from the fact that this atmospheric old hostelry originally provided refreshments for Crusaders setting off for the Holy Land.

In 1330 Edward III entered Nottingham Castle through the inn when he came to arrest his mother's lover, Roger Mortimer, Earl of March, who had been responsible for the horrific murder of his father, Edward II, in 1327. Mortimer was captured in the royal apartment. Ignoring the pleas of his mother, Isabella, to 'have pity on the gentle Mortimer', Edward had him dragged to the Tower of London and then executed at Tyburn. Isabella's ghostly entreaties are still said to sound from the depths of the rock, and ghostly footsteps are often heard pacing around the stark caverns that form the pub's cellars (which can be visited with the landlord's permission).

Opposite: Claiming to be the oldest inn in England, Nottingham's Ye Olde Trip to Jerusalem is home to a sinister artifact the cleaning of which brings bad luck.

WELSH BORDERS & PEAK DISTRICT

DERBYSHIRE, STAFFORDSHIRE, CHESHIRE & SHROPSHIRE

The Lion and Swan Hotel, Congleton, Cheshire – see page 110

The female ghost appears in the early hours of the morning and can be seen tending the fire, wearing nothing but clogs and a winsome smile.

This is a region of dramatic contrasts. It is where the untamed splendour of Derbyshire's Peak District gives way to the gentle pastures and valleys of Staffordshire and Cheshire, which in turn roll into the Shropshire countryside. The latter's tranquil landscapes belie a stormy past: its proximity to the border with Wales meant that its inhabitants lived under the constant threat of a Welsh uprising. Needless to say, the region's old inns and hotels are haunted by a rich and varied array of spectres. Ghostly Cavaliers, jilted brides and other tragic figures often materialize before the living to chill the marrow and tingle the spine. The Whittington Inn at Kinver can boast the area's most illustrious ghost in the form of Lady Jane Grey, but the prize for the most tantalizing revenant must surely go to the naked spectre that pokes the fire at Congleton's Lion and Swan Hotel! All in all the delightful variety of inns in these counties makes for an intriguing and rewarding journey.

1. The Castle Hotel
2. The Red Lion Inn
3. The Eyre Arms
4. The Whittington Inn
5. Ye Olde Dog and Partridge
6. Lion and Swan Hotel
7. Ye Olde King's Head
8. The Prince Rupert Hotel
9. The Acton Arms
10. The Tontine Hotel

THE CASTLE HOTEL
The jilted bride and the spectral old man

THE CASTLE HOTEL ⌖✗
CASTLE STREET, CASTLETON
HOPE VALLEY, DERBYSHIRE
TEL: 01433 620578

Castleton is a large village, magnificently situated at the western end of the Peak District's awesomely beautiful Hope Valley. It is dominated by the imposing ruin of Peveril Castle and lies within the shadow of Mam Tor, also known as the 'Shivering Mountain' on account of the eroded shale that falls from its slopes into the valley below. There are also numerous caves to explore in the immediate vicinity. Visitors need a place to stay, and the stone-built Castle Hotel, with its beamed interior and cosy atmosphere, offers bed and breakfast – and the management are happy to throw in four ghosts at no extra charge.

The most active of the inn's spectral inhabitants is the ghostly housekeeper, Agnes. Witnesses describe her as being about 60 years old, around 5 feet 4 inches (1.6 metres) tall, a little on the plump side, with grey hair, which she keeps tied back into a bun. She wanders the upstairs corridors, apparently intent on keeping a concerned eye on the well-being of patrons. Such is her devotion to duty that guests regularly enjoy the novel experience of being tucked in by her phantom form at night!

A second wraith is that of an unfortunate bride, jilted on her wedding day by a feckless lover. Tradition holds that her reception was to be held at The Castle Hotel and she, therefore, committed suicide in room 4. Her grief has rendered her spirit earthbound and her sad shade, resplendent in a flowing white dress, has been seen at several locations around the property.

The third ghost is that of a regular from the early years of the 20th century. Since his wife wasn't keen on his drinking, he would sneak into the bar via the side entrance in order that as few people as possible would see him and report back to his good lady. By trade he was miner, and so only ever wore a suit on Sundays. It was during a furtive Sabbath visit that he suddenly dropped dead at the bar where his dapper shade, dressed in a blue pinstriped suit, has been condemned to remain ever since. In May 1999 a female guest went to the ladies' toilet (which stands where the side entrance used to be) and she was confronted by a well-groomed phantom figure that proceeded to pass right through her.

The fourth ghost is of greater antiquity, though not seen as frequently as his companions. He is a soldier dressed in the regalia of the time of Charles II.

Opposite: Visitors to the Castle Hotel in Castleton may well be treated to the unique experience of being tucked in at night by an elderly ghostly housekeeper.

Most witnesses say that he seems to be very angry about something. But what is most disturbing about this particular apparition is that he is only ever visible from the knees up. The reason for this is that, over the centuries, the floor and ceiling levels have been altered, and his feet remain firmly planted on the level he would have known in life!

THE RED LION INN
The dishevelled spectre

THE RED LION INN ⊨✕
MAIN STREET, HOGNASTON
ASHBOURNE, DERBYSHIRE
TEL: 01335 370396

Nestling at the heart of the picturesque village of Hognaston, the 17th-entury Red Lion Inn is a cosy and pleasant retreat that can lift the spirits of even the most world-weary traveller. It is such an appealing place that at least two of its former patrons have shown a marked reluctance to pass on. The most frequently seen entity is a man in his early middle ages, with a military bearing and dressed in what witnesses have described as a World War I army greatcoat, resplendent with shiny brass buttons. His hair is longer than one might expect and his appearance is said to be somewhat dishevelled. Who he is and why he chooses to roam the pub is not known. An old man who wears a flat cap and holds a walking stick regularly joins him. He often comes strolling up to the old back entrance of the inn (which is now located inside the building), and upon reaching it abruptly melts away into thin air. Landlady Pip Price, who has experienced the spectral roving of both ghosts, believes him to have been a regular of the pub who is not going to let a little thing like death stand between him and a visit to a place for which he evidently had great affection.

THE EYRE ARMS
The ghostly Cavalier

THE EYRE ARMS ✕
HASSOP, BAKEWELL, DERBYSHIRE
TEL: 01629 640390

The Eyre Arms is a delightful and unspoilt 17th-century inn, resplendent with original oak beams, stone walls and a splendid grandfather clock in the lounge. At the back, it can also boast an old leper shelf, where those afflicted with the dreadful contagion could deposit their ale money in tankards of vinegar and, in so doing, cleanse it of all traces of the disease.

A ghostly Cavalier, whose origins go back to the dark days of the Civil War, haunts the pub. One day, so the story goes, he was hiding in the roof space when a gaggle of rowdy Roundheads learned of his whereabouts and set out to capture him. Drawing his rapier, he put up a good fight and even managed to drive his attackers back to the staircase which, in those days, stretched from the middle of the pub to the front door. But here he was overpowered and the Parliamentarians fell upon him, plunging their swords relentlessly into him until, with a deep gasp, the poor man expired. Today customers occasionally catch fleeting glimpses of his wandering wraith behind the bar that now stands on the site of the old staircase on which the bold Cavalier left his mark forever.

THE WHITTINGTON INN
Lady Jane Grey's icy spectre

The timbered walls of this magnificent hostelry are steeped in history, and its splendid interior of beams, panelling and open fires creates an atmosphere that evokes a more genteel age. Sir William de Whittenton, grandfather of

> THE WHITTINGTON INN ✕
> WHITTINGTON KINVER
> STOWBRIDGE, WEST MIDLANDS
> TEL: 01384 872110

Dick Whittington, built it in 1310. The family had only been in residence for 40 years when William's son, William, incurred royal censure by marrying a nobleman's widow without the King's consent. He was forced to sell his Kinver estate and move to Gloucestershire from where, in due course, his famous son set out for London.

The house's new owners, the de La Lowes, married into the Grey family. As a result the building acquired its illustrious ghost in the 16th century, when their most famous member, Lady Jane Grey – the so-called 'nine-day queen' – spent some of her childhood here. Such was her liking for the old manor that, following her execution in 1554, her spirit returned to it and has remained in residence ever since. Her footsteps have been heard pacing along the upstairs corridors at dead of night, and people have mentioned sensing her 'presence' at sundry locations about the property.

Over the years other noble guests followed in Lady Jane's physical, though not psychical, footsteps. Charles II spent a night at the old house in September 1651, following his defeat at the Battle of Worcester. Later, Queen Anne paid a visit and left behind her royal seal, which can still be seen on the pub's door. In 1783 the Lord of the Manor, Lord Stamford and Warrington, acquired both the licence and the sign of the nearby Whittington Inn,

transferred them to his manor house and converted the property into the atmospheric inn that it remains today.

Over the years the inn has managed to acquire a few more spectral inhabitants. A pressure on the bed, as though someone were leaning over it, has woken several people sleeping there in the past. Moments later, they have been gripped round the throat by clammy, though invisible, hands. Unable to cry out or move, the hapless victims have had little choice but to endure their ordeal for what seems like an eternity until, come dawn, their invisible assailant finally releases its grip.

A party of diners in the appropriately named 'Lady Jane's Room' was startled one night when a door handle began to move. Although the door remained closed, they all felt the temperature drop alarmingly. Suddenly the handle on the opposite door began to turn, and although that door also remained closed, the temperature returned to normal as their unseen guest apparently left the room.

YE OLDE DOG AND PARTRIDGE
Gracie's restless wraith

The building now known as Ye Olde Dog and Partridge dates from around 1440, although it did not become an inn until 1754. The ghost of a young girl, about 11 years old, haunts it. No one is entirely certain who she was or

YE OLDE DOG AND PARTRIDGE 🛏️🍴
HIGH STREET, TUTBURY
BURTON-ON-TRENT, STAFFORDSHIRE
TEL: 01283 813030

when she lived, but staff and customers have come to know her affectionately as Gracie. A local tradition that Gracie was hanged in room 33 of the hotel is nigh on impossible to substantiate. But in the absence of an alternative explanation as to why her wraith roams the premises, this is the reason most often given. What is certain is that her ghost is benign, happy to sing, skip and indulge in other harmless childish pursuits, such as bouncing a phantom ball against walls in the dead of night. Doors that open and close, apparently of their own volition, are attributed to her, as are the objects that regularly and mysteriously get moved from one place to another. She has also been known to indulge in a little prankish poltergeist activity, such as lifting full beer glasses off the bar's counter and tipping the contents on the floor. But annoying as her

Opposite: Shrewsbury's Prince Rupert Hotel is the spectral haunt of a lady who seeks a husband and a jilted husband who seeks a bride. Sadly, though, the two have never met!

visits can sometimes prove, there is not a living soul that wishes her ill, and she is allowed to wander at will, as she has for as long as anyone can remember.

LION AND SWAN HOTEL
The naked lady at the fireside

LION AND SWAN HOTEL 🛏️✕
SWAN BANK
CONGLETON, CHESHIRE
TEL: 01260 273115

The timbered façade of the Lion and Swan Hotel, once a popular coaching inn for travellers bound for Manchester, is sited in the attractive market town of Congleton. Dating in part from the early 15th century, one of the building's most intriguing features is the ornately carved fireplace in the restaurant. Lions, together with fruits of a decidedly erotic appearance, are featured, as is a group of four figures of questionable gender. There is a tradition that the panels on which the carvings are depicted may once have been the ends of a bridal bed, and that the sensual imagery was intended as a fertility aid for barren couples.

It is therefore only right that the hotel's female ghost should choose to appear in the vicinity of the fireplace, manifesting herself in the early hours of the morning, around the time of the full moon, apparently tending the fire beneath the carvings. Her most endearing trait, however, is the fact that, apart from a pair of clogs on her feet, and a winsome smile on her face, she is stark naked.

No one knows for certain who she was or when she lived, although there is a tradition that she died in the latter part of the Middle Ages, possibly poisoned by a love potion she had enthusiastically, though fatally, imbibed. She must be one of the more unusual of England's female phantoms. After all, grey ladies, white ladies, blue, green and pink ladies abound upon our spectral shores, but a nude lady with clogs on – that's different!

YE OLDE KING'S HEAD
The crying child and the writing on the mirror

YE OLDE KING'S HEAD 🛏️✕
48–50 LOWER BRIDGE STREET
CHESTER, CHESHIRE
TEL: 01244 324855

Dating from 1520 and boasting a magnificent black-and-white timber-framed frontage, Ye Olde King's Head is one of Chester's oldest hotels. Its dark, low-beamed interior with wooden partitions, stained-glass panels and time-worn pews is truly convivial and atmospheric. It comes as little surprise to learn that this ancient hostelry has a few otherworldly inhabitants, whose comings and goings occasionally cross with those of living residents.

Guests in room 6, the Daresbury Room, have spoken of an icy breeze blowing across them from the wall to the right of the four-poster bed. What is particularly unnerving is that this is sometimes accompanied by the sound of a baby crying, even when no children are staying at the hotel. In room 4, meanwhile, an invisible ghost has been known to communicate with guests by writing messages on the bathroom mirror.

Another part of the hotel with a reputation for strange phenomena is the restaurant, where unseen hands have the annoying habit of rearranging and moving utensils, much to the mystification of the waiters and waitresses. But on the whole, the ghosts that haunt Ye Olde King's Head are an ambivalent bunch and their presence adds to, rather than detracts from, the overall ambience of the building. Indeed, such is the blend of old world atmosphere and new world comforts here that it would prove a great disappointment were you to discover that this place of creaking floorboards and dark corners *wasn't* haunted!

THE PRINCE RUPERT HOTEL
The spectral lonely hearts

This delightful old building is named for Prince Rupert, grandson of James I and nephew of the ill-fated Charles I. It was his private residence during the English Civil War, and its timber-framed walls

THE PRINCE RUPERT HOTEL 🛏🍴
BUTCHER ROW
SHREWSBURY, SHROPSHIRE
TEL: 01743 499955

and oak-beamed rooms resound with history.

In 1991 a medium staying in rooms 4 and 5 (the honeymoon suite) completed a guest questionnaire and offered an intriguing challenge to customer services. 'These spirits kept me awake most nights,' she wrote, 'and the sudden changes in atmosphere when going from one part of the hotel to another are quite unnecessary. May I recommend that when the refurbishment is absolutely complete you get the hotel blessed by a local vicar.' She claimed that the renovations then taking place in the 15th-century section of the property had disturbed the ghosts of several former residents, including someone who had either been buried in the cellar or bricked up behind one of the old walls.

Although this particular revenant's resting place still remains a mystery, an abundance of other spectres are known to wander the hotel. A spectral man is said to appear in room 7 and to walk along the corridor outside. He is reputed to have hanged himself when his fiancée eloped with his best man shortly before they were due to be married. He now searches for them during the hours of darkness, although whether his motivation is reunion or revenge is unknown. He might be better off letting bygones be bygones and diverting his time-worn path into room 6, said to be haunted by the wraith of a young woman who seeks a man to marry her! Ghostly voices heard chatting in the night, the feeling of cold breath on guests' cheeks, depressions suddenly appearing at the end of a bed as though someone has just sat down, and a spectral man in period costume sitting in a chair at the entrance to the Prince Rupert Lounge – are just some of the other phenomena experienced by visitors to this lovely old place where the walls just crackle with atmosphere.

THE ACTON ARMS
He vaguely resembles a man

THE ACTON ARMS 🍽✕
HAUGHTON LANE, MORVILLE
NR BRIDGNORTH, SHROPSHIRE
TEL: 01746 714209

The Acton Arms is haunted by an enigmatic male spectre of regular habits whose origins lie lost in the mists of time. All anybody knows is that, in life, he was a monk who at some unspecified time in history committed an indiscretion that resulted in him breaking one or more of his vows. There is talk of a secret tunnel that once connected the pub with the church across the road, and it has been rumoured that the lustful friar used this passage to enjoy illicit liaisons with a local lady. Whether, when caught, he did the honourable thing and committed suicide, or suffered the time-honoured fate of being bricked up alive behind a wall of the pub as punishment, is unknown. What is certain, however, is that in the past his ghost was a very busy one.

One landlady, Mary Walker, who claimed to have seen him on an almost daily basis, described him as 'a white shape, vaguely in the form of a man'. She went on to say how, when she entered a particular room, she would often find him sitting or crouching in there. But the moment he became aware of her presence, he had the annoying habit of whisking away before her very eyes.

THE TONTINE HOTEL
Murder most foul

The Ironbridge Gorge was one of the major centres in Britain's Industrial Revolution, and the 200-foot (60-metre) bridge that spans the River Severn – and after which it was named – marked the first use of iron in industrial archi-

> THE TONTINE HOTEL
> THE SQUARE, IRONBRIDGE
> TELFORD, SHROPSHIRE
> TEL: 01952 432127

tecture. It was constructed in 1779, and The Tontine Hotel was built opposite six years later.

This splendid, cosy hotel is the haunt of a restless wraith, thought to be that of one of the last men to be hanged in Shropshire. On 6 September 1950, 40-year-old Frank Griffin robbed and murdered Mrs Jane Edge, a 74-year-old landlady from Ketley. Having fled the scene, he took refuge in room 5 of the Tontine Hotel, where the police caught up with him. Griffin was arrested, tried for murder, found guilty, and on 4 January 1951 was executed in Shrewsbury.

Perhaps it is his anxiety in those final moments of freedom that have left behind a psychic imprint on the room, for many guests staying there have commented on feeling a 'presence'. A maintenance man was working in the room in 2001, using an industrial lamp and a drill, plugged into a dual socket. Suddenly the temperature began to drop alarmingly and, as it did so, all the lights went out, as did the lamp. Yet the drill, plugged into the same power point, continued to work. Unnerved, the man fled from the room and refused to enter it again unless there was someone else with him. It is quite common for guests to experience a drop in temperature in room 5, and in the past, lights and taps have switched on and off of their own accord. It has also been known for clock hands to mysteriously run backwards in front of astonished witnesses.

A mother and daughter, whose family were occupying another bedroom, saw the ghost of a little girl in a smock frock standing in the corner of their room. Interestingly, the rest of the family remained oblivious to the presence of their ghostly visitor, and it was only when a look of puzzlement crossed the faces of the two females that they realized anything was amiss. This, however, appears to have been an isolated ghostly incident, and the girl's identity remains one of the many secrets of which a building of such antiquity inevitably remains a formidable guardian.

THE NORTH
YORKSHIRE, LANCASHIRE, CUMBRIA & NORTHUMBERLAND

Lord Crewe Arms Hotel, Blanchland, Hexham, County Durham – see page 124
*Dorothy implores a guest in the Bamburgh Room to take a message
to her brother in France.*

You can't fail to be moved by the scenic variety of these northern counties, and the haunted inns found here reflect this ever-changing panorama. North of the urban spread of Lancashire is the awesome majesty of the Lake District, where you feel as if you are standing on the roof of the country. Set in the brooding mountains of Lakeland are hostelries that, in the past, were the very embodiment of a wayside inn. Many a traveller, caught in a sudden snowstorm or dense fog, must have owed his or her survival to these remote refuges – although many have shown their gratitude by returning as ghosts! Elsewhere the picturesque inns of the Yorkshire Dales provide a striking contrast to the solid grey walls of the austere pubs along the wild and untamed Northumberland coast. The stories of many of the ghosts that haunt these inns reflect the stormy past of this border region, which witnessed frequent bloody skirmishes over the much-disputed boundary with Scotland.

1. The Red Lion Hotel
2. The Goat Gap Inn
3. Ye Olde Starre Inne
4. The Old Silent Inn
5. The Pack Horse
6. The Royal Oak Inn
7. The Kirkstone Pass Inn
8. Lord Crewe Arms Hotel
9. The Famous Schooner Hotel

BEER GARDEN

YE
OLDE STARRE INNE

YORK'S OLDEST
LICENSED INN 1644

THE RED LION HOTEL
The entity and the psychic

Originally a 16th-century ferryman's inn, The Red Lion has developed around the original structure and is now a lovely, cosy riverside hostelry. An intriguing feature is the horse trough, which once stood outside the old

> THE RED LION HOTEL
> BY THE BRIDGE, BURNSALL
> NR SKIPTON, NORTH YORKSHIRE
> TEL: 01756 720204

building but which now resides under the stone steps leading to the bedrooms. Why is it there? Simply because it was easier to build around it than to attempt to move it!

Liz Grayshon, proprietor of The Red Lion, readily acknowledges that her inn is haunted. 'We have always known there was an entity here,' she told me. 'But matters came to a head when a new member of staff who was psychic was zoomed in on and really pestered.' Liz and her staff, however, were able to use this opportunity to find out more about their 'presence', and learnt that he was the ghost of a former resident who had committed suicide and been buried in unconsecrated ground outside the churchyard. 'I don't really talk about or think about him much,' observes Liz, 'as that causes him to "come to me".'

While she was responding to my e-mail asking for clarification on a few points about the ghost, she mentioned that, 'as I am writing, the office is becoming quite chilly'.

Eventually the local diocese agreed to send someone who specializes in laying unquiet spirits, and a committal service was held. It seems to have done the trick for, as Liz later informed me, 'This has, for the main part, quietened him'.

THE GOAT GAP INN
Ring a ring a roses

Situated on a tract of bleak moorland on one of the A65's loneliest stretches, this whitewashed stone inn – with its low-beamed, narrow corridors, dark interior, and helicopter landing pad for those who

> THE GOAT GAP INN
> GIGGLESWICK, NORTH YORKSHIRE
> TEL: 015 242 41230

wish to, literally, 'drop in' for a pint – has a long tradition of being haunted.

Opposite: As York's oldest inn, Ye Olde Starre, has many a ghost to chill the blood; however, the antics of its spectral cats have caused a few headaches to canine visitors.

So many ghosts had apparently chosen to linger here that in the early 1990s it was deemed necessary to clear out some of the surplus ghostly population, and an exorcism was performed. Several unwelcome phantoms were dispatched, including a demon found sitting on a banister.

But every old inn should have a resident ghost or two, and so several were allowed to remain. In the Burnmoor Room guests have watched in stunned silence as an invisible hand slowly turns the handle of the hot tap. In another room residents have been disturbed by the sounds of childish voices singing 'Ring a ring a roses'.

The downstairs bar is the haunt of a cloth-capped, ghostly drover whom successive landlords have christened 'George', believed to be a former owner of the property when the remote wayside inn was a tiny farmhouse. He sits pensively in a corner by the window, his unblinking eyes gazing fixedly ahead, staring at nothing in particular. He bothers no one, and no one bothers him, as he occupies a favoured position much as he may have done long ago in life, content to watch the world pass by.

YE OLDE STARRE INNE
Beware the phantom dog

YE OLDE STARRE INNE ✗
40 STONEGATE
YORK, NORTH YORKSHIRE
TEL: 01904 623063

York is widely considered to be England's most haunted city and close on 140 ghosts are said to exist cheek by jowl with its living populace. It has many a haunted inn, but the one that boasts the most unusual ghostly activity is Ye Olde Starre Inne, the oldest pub in the city.

It dates back to 1644, although the cellar may be much older, possibly even 10th century. William Foster, landlord during the English Civil War, was a staunch Royalist and was none too pleased when a bunch of Parliamentarian Roundheads popped in for pint one day. During that same conflict the cellar was used as an operating room for Royalists wounded during the battle of nearby Marston Moor. The screams and groans of the dead and dying are still said to echo through the premises in the early hours of some mornings. Another ghost is that of an old woman in black, who ascends the staircase from time to time. Her identity is just one of many secrets to which a place of this antiquity is privy, and since she is only ever visible to very young children descriptions of her tend to be somewhat vague.

However, the most unusual spirits are those of two black cats who were, reputedly, bricked up alive in the pillar between the door and the bar. It was once quite common to brick up live cats in the walls or foundations of a building since their presence was believed to ward off both ill luck and fire. Such insurance was anything but lucky for the unfortunate felines, whose ghosts often protest loudly against such injustice. Often their phantom forms can be heard scampering around the pub at night. Dogs seem to be a favoured butt of their spectral attention, and many is the canine who snarls and bristles at 'something'. One poor pooch, brave enough to attack the invisible presence, was rendered unconscious when he suddenly leapt forward and slammed head first into the pillar where the cats are said to repose!

THE OLD SILENT INN
The ghostly cat lover

The evocative name of this delightful old inn trips off the tongue and conjures up haunting and romantic images of mystery and antiquity. It is surrounded by remote and awesomely beautiful moorland made famous by the Brontë

THE OLD SILENT INN 🛏 ✕
HOB LANE, STANBURY
KEIGHLEY, WEST YORKSHIRE
TEL: 01535 647437

sisters, who lived at nearby Haworth. Records show that the building is over 400 years old and that the inn was originally known as The Eagle on account of the fact that eagles once soared over this wild and rugged landscape.

There are two legends as to how the weathered old hostelry came by its current name. One holds that a traveller was murdered in the vicinity and his body flung into a nearby stream. When the officers of the law arrived to investigate the killing, the locals refused to name the culprits, from which silence the name of the inn was derived.

The other, more romantic, tale tells how Bonnie Prince Charlie, the Young Pretender, paid the inn a visit during the 1745 Jacobean uprising and stayed for several weeks. The villagers were told to 'Keep silent' about their illustrious guest's presence, and hence the name of the pub was changed to commemorate their refusal to betray their royal patron.

The Old Silent Inn cries out to be haunted, and several of those who have crossed its threshold in the past have taken it upon themselves to ensure that the dedicated ghost-hunter who comes in search of a little haunted hospitality does not leave disappointed.

A headless soldier who traipses across the bar, and a large male figure that trudges endlessley up and down the stairs, are two of the more regular phantoms. But it is the sound of what appears to be a small hand bell tinkling in the distance that has become the most consistent and best-attested haunting at The Old Silent Inn.

Tradition holds that a long a time ago a kindly old landlady provided food for the wild cats that foraged amidst the unforgiving terrain of the surrounding moors. She would announce feeding time by ringing a little bell from a doorway of the inn that has since been blocked up, and this is where the ghostly tinkling is now heard. It is also where, from time to time, staff and customers have caught fleeting glimpses of a little old woman, seen gazing out towards the moors for a few moments before she melts away into thin air.

THE PACK HORSE
Skulduggery at the bar

THE PACK HORSE ✕
52 WATLING STREET
AFFETSIDE, BURY LANCASTER
TEL: 01204 883802

The road that runs across the exposed moorland hilltop on which The Pack Horse stands was laid out by the Romans around AD79 and formed part of Watling Street. The stone pillar, known as the Affetside Cross, that stands nearby is said to mark the exact halfway spot between London and Edinburgh, although the claim that it is of Roman origin is dubious. The Pack Horse possibly dates from 1443, and its heyday came in the 18th century when it serviced the needs of the packhorse trains that plodded their way along the dusty byways of the region. At the end of the century a new turnpike road bypassed the village, and The Pack Horse's days of glory were over.

In the last 200 years The Pack Horse has evolved into a cosy and welcoming hostelry. But many of the visitors who pitch up at its weathered walls are drawn not by its hospitality but by the chance of acquainting themselves with its most famous resident, a battered old skull, tobacco-stained and very delicate, that leers at them from a shelf behind the bar. It is said to have belonged to Affetside man George Wherwell.

In 1651, during the English Civil War, James, 7th Earl of Derby, commanded the Royalist troops who were responsible for the massacre of Bolton. Having been caught, the Earl was sentenced to be beheaded, and George Wherwell – whose family had been victims of the Royalists – volunteered as his executioner. His vengeance, however, was short-lived, for

Opposite: Bad luck and fearsome apparitions await anyone who tempts to remove the resident skull from the confines of Affetside's Pack Horse inn.

the Royalists caught up with him and meted out a similar retribution. His head was displayed on a pike outside The Pack Horse, to serve as a warning to others who might be contemplating a career as a headsman. When the flesh had rotted away, the skull was brought inside the pub and has remained here ever since.

There are many tales concerning the misfortunes that have befallen anyone who has tried to remove the skull from The Pack Horse. A customer with the wonderful name of Siah Slopp once stole it as a drunken prank. In the middle of the night a ferocious knocking at the door woke the pub's landlord. Opening it he found a terrified Siah, holding the skull and begging him to take it back. He recounted how he had put the skull on his bedside table, but no sooner had he fallen asleep than a blow on the nose jolted him from his slumber. Opening his eyes he saw what appeared to be a 'giant moth of a ghostly blue colour' with blazing red eyes floating before him. It was the skull, and as he lay there petrified, a blood curdling voice ordered him to, 'Tak' me back to where I should be, or I'll tormen' thy soul out of thee!' Siah didn't need telling a second time and, leaping out of bed, he returned the skull to The Pack Horse.

Now it so happened that the landlord mentioned the episode to three of his regulars. They didn't believe him, and stole the skull in order to see if a similar fate would befall them. As they made their way along the road, clutching their quarry, a spectral executioner wielding a murderous-looking axe suddenly appeared before them. 'Tak' that skull back or I'll chop thy silly yed off,' screamed the fearful apparition. Then, in a rare display of spirit humour, it pointed the axe towards them and punned, 'If I have to ax thee again I'st axe thee wi' this'. Not surprisingly they didn't hang around to see if the phantom would carry out his threat, but quickly returned the skull to its rightful home at The Pack Horse inn. And there it remains to this day, a curious relic whose hollow eyes keep a constant watch on the comings and goings of the Pack Horse's clientele.

THE ROYAL OAK INN
The Dobbie's resident spirit

THE ROYAL OAK INN 🛏 ✗
BONGATE, APPLEBY-IN-
WESTMORLAND, CUMBRIA
TEL: 01768 351463

This 17th-century coaching inn began life as just one room, and was then gradually extended into the long, low, whitewashed building that it is today. It is the sort of place in which you can happily while away either a summer's afternoon or a wind-tossed winter's evening and, should haunted fortune smile upon you, you may even be blessed with a sighting of one of the three resident ghosts.

The inn is the haunt of a spectral child who has been known to sit on the end of guests' beds and chat happily with them. So real does this juvenile revenant appear that guests will happily converse, not realizing that the child is anything other than flesh and blood. Until, that is, they turn away momentarily, and on turning back find that the child has disappeared.

Equally mysterious, though probably of greater antiquity, is the 'Dobbie' who has been seen several times in one of the bedrooms. In local folklore a 'Dobbie' is a household fairy that attaches itself to a favoured family. As long as a bowl of milk and an oaten cake are left out for the little fellow at night, he will ensure the smooth running of the household and even help the servants with their tasks. Failure to adhere to his simple demands, however, can have the opposite effect, with cooking being disrupted, or the work of the day, such as weaving, sewing and washing, being spoilt during the night.

The final ghost on the premises is that of an old man who is seen in the restaurant. He is reputedly a former tenant from the days when the building was a private house, and since he 'doesn't do much, apart from sit by the fire' the inn's manager Jo Collins is happy to leave him be and just accept him as the oldest resident of her atmospheric hostelry.

THE KIRKSTONE PASS INN
Lakeland's highest haunted inn

The Kirkstone Pass, at 1489 feet (453 metres), is the highest road pass in the Lake District. It confronts the intrepid traveller with an uncompromising kaleidoscope of untamed mountain splendour,

THE KIRKSTONE PASS INN ⊨ ✗
PATTERDALE ROAD, KIRKSTONE PASS
NR AMBLESIDE, CUMBRIA
TEL: 01539 433624

mysterious pools and demonic bleak sedges. It is Lakeland wilderness at its best – or worst, depending on your view. It is also the unlikely location for what is, without doubt, one of England's most atmospheric old inns.

The Kirkstone Pass Inn is the highest of all Lakeland's inns, and affords stunning views over the dark waters of Windermere, shimmering in the valley far below. The little whitewashed building dates in part from 1496 when it was appropriately known as The Travellers Rest. The building was extended in the mid 19th century, and renamed The Kirkstone Pass Inn. It has hardly changed since, and for the jaded 21st-century city dweller there is no better place to *really* get away from it all.

The inn is self-sufficient as far as power and water go – it would just about bankrupt any utility company that tried to run cables or pipes up to its lofty heights. At night warm fires blaze in the ancient grates, candles cast shadows across the old walls, and as the silence of the fells envelopes the little hostelry, the atmosphere becomes wonderfully conducive to the telling of ghost stories.

Several chilling tales come marching from the mist-shrouded past of The Kirkstone Pass Inn. There is the woman, known simply as Ruth, who one day set out with her baby to pay a visit to her sick father. En route she was caught in a blizzard. Having wrapped her child in her shawl to protect it against the driving snow, she stumbled onwards, but eventually the storm overcame her and she died of exposure. The baby survived, and ever since the mother's revenant has wandered the night hours on an eternal quest to be reunited with her child.

Then there is the ghost of a little boy called Neville, a mischievous sprite who takes pictures off the walls and generally makes a nuisance of himself. Tradition holds that he was run over and killed by a coach and horses directly outside the inn.

An 18th-century landlord was lynched by the locals and strung up on a 'hanging tree', reputedly following the disappearance of his two children. It is said that this same tree was then pressed into regular service for the dispatching of other felons, and that numerous people sense the unquiet spirits of those who were hanged.

Finally, there is the ghost of Benjamin the coachman. Several members of staff have caught ethereal glimpses of a large man moving around the darker recesses of the old inn. A visitor who got his family to pose in the porch for a photograph was most perturbed to see that when the film was developed the figure of a man – who had certainly not been there when the picture was taken – could clearly be seen in the background.

LORD CREWE ARMS HOTEL
Dorothy Forster's eternal search

LORD CREWE ARMS HOTEL 🛏 ✕
BLANCHLAND, HEXHAM
COUNTY DURHAM
TEL: 01434 675251

The sleepy ambience of Blanchland village evokes a poignant nostalgia for a slower-paced, more genteel age. Its 18th-century stone cottages are laid out along the foundations of Blanchland Abbey, to whose plan the village remains true, and its rustic charm is complemented by an almost Mediterranean appearance.

The abbey was founded in AD1165 by the Premonstratensian order, whose distinctive white habits gave the village its name 'Blancalande', or White Land. Its isolated location meant that daily life was a constant struggle, compounded by the danger of savage raids from the 'border reivers'.

One day a party of these feared and ferocious outlaws is said to have set out for the abbey intent on murder, pillage and plunder. The monks received word of their approach and prepared for it as best they could. However, suddenly a dense fog descended, causing all in the raiding party to become disorientated. Convinced that this was nothing short of divine intervention, the monks gave thanks by letting out a joyous peal of the abbey bells. It was an ill-conceived act of piety: their would-be attackers simply followed the sound and massacred all the monks. On certain days of the year, the bells of the village church are said to ring of their own accord as the misty wraiths of the murdered monks are seen around the churchyard.

Next door to the church is what must surely count as one of England's cosiest and most characterful establishments, The Lord Crewe Arms Hotel. It was formerly the abbot's guest house and its ancient stone walls, barrel-vaulted crypt bar, low-beamed ceilings and massive fireplaces, one of which contains a cleverly concealed 'priest's hide', positively crackle with atmosphere.

A building of such impressive antiquity inevitably harbours several ghosts behind its inviting façade. An American guest, sleeping in the Radcliffe Room in the late 1990s, awoke in the early hours of one morning to find a monk dressed in a white habit kneeling at the end of the four-poster bed. Unperturbed by the apparition, she reached down and touched it, finding him to be 'quite solid'. But no sooner had she done so than he became hazy and slowly melted away.

But the hotel's best-known ghost is that of Dorothy Forster, who appears to have a penchant for the Bamburgh Room. She was the sister of Tom Forster, the unwilling commander of the Jacobite forces during the 1715 uprising. Poor Tom had no qualifications (and even fewer natural instincts) for such an important position and, when confronted by his adversaries at Preston, surrendered without even attempting to fight. Taken to London and incarcerated in Newgate Prison, Tom awaited his inevitable fate. But his devoted sister Dorothy succeeded in engineering his escape just three days before he was due to stand trial for high treason. She had him brought to The Lord Crewe Arms and kept hidden in the priest's hide behind the fireplace until it was deemed safe to smuggle him out of the country to France.

Sadly, brother and sister never saw each other again, for Tom Forster died in France. Dorothy stayed behind at The Lord Crewe Arms and has remained here ever since. Many is the night that guests sleeping in the Bamburgh Room have been woken by her sad spectre imploring them to take a message to her brother in France, telling him that all is now well and he can safely return to England.

THE FAMOUS SCHOONER HOTEL
Ghosts galore!

THE FAMOUS SCHOONER HOTEL 🛏 ✕
NORTHUMBERLAND STREET
ALNMOUTH, NORTHUMBERLAND
TEL: 01665 830216

The plain white exterior of this 17th-century coaching inn belies an interior that teems with 'olde worlde' charm and a veritable array of ghosts. There is the ghostly lady who wanders the first-floor corridor in the early hours, tapping upon walls and doors. Elsewhere hotel guests have been awoken in the night by the sound of gasping and choking that appear to be coming from the floor beside their bed, but can see no one. According to local tradition, Rose Llewellyn, wife of the landlord, was beaten and strangled in her room in 1809, and her spectral death throes still echo down the centuries.

The wispy silhouette of a spectral lady who fixes witnesses with a sad gaze and then melts away into thin air is another ghostly inhabitant. An alarming drop in temperature always accompanies her appearances. Her identity is unknown, although there is a faint possibility that she may be connected to another particularly gruesome murder.

In the late 17th century the landlord, Bill Wilson, hacked his wife and two children to death with a meat cleaver. It is convenient speculation to associate the wispy lady with the murdered wife, but her nocturnal wanderings are often accompanied by childish sobbing resonating through the upper sections of the inn.

However, the best-known ghost is that of Parson Smyth, an 18th-century clergyman whose ruddy complexion spoke volumes about his fondness for the demon drink. In 1742 the landlord, John Duchar, began brewing a particularly potent ale and, anxious to win the approval of the dipsomaniacal vicar, obligingly sent him a keg of the new brew. Unfortunately, as Parson Smyth excitedly opened the cask, he was struck on the head by the tap and killed instantly. The offending tap was duly returned to the inn, but no one ever dared use it again for fear it would flow with the parson's blood. Likewise, Smyth's tragic demise sounded the death knell for the new ale, since people thought it might bring them similar bad luck. Parson Smyth, resplendent in a black cloak and, no doubt, nursing an almighty hangover, has drifted about the lower levels of the premises ever since, holding the offending tap high for all to see, before disappearing into the nearest wall.

Many more ghosts are known to walk the corridors of this superb old inn, and in recent years it has become something of a Mecca for ghost-hunting societies and enthusiasts. Such is the regularity of supernatural phenomenon at The Famous Schooner that those who come here in search of things mysterious rarely leave disappointed.

WALES

MONMOUTHSHIRE, DENBIGHSHIRE, GLAMORGAN, WREXHAM, CONWY, GWYNEDD & PEMBROKESHIRE

The Rhos Fynach Pub and Restaurant, Rhos-on-Sea, Colwyn Bay, Conwy – see page 137
The stolen Christmas tree, complete with baubles, tinsel and ribbon, was found standing at the pub's entrance – with a note attached.

Starting with what I consider to be one creepiest pubs I have ever visited, The Skirrid Mountain Inn, the Welsh leg of my journey provided some wonderful surprises. I set out with hardly any idea of which places were haunted and so had to, literally, stop off at inns and ask if they had a resident phantom! Luckily my researches bore fruit and I came across a nice variety of haunted hostelries. Ghostly ladies of different hues tended to be the most active of the wraiths to inhabit Welsh inns, but they were more than complemented by an abundance of other typical inexplicable phenomena, such as lights being turned on and off and objects mysteriously disappearing. But of all the stories I uncovered I must confess that the one that delighted me the most was the report of the thieving monk who may have been responsible for almost ruining the Christmas festivities at the Rhos Fynach Pub in December 2002.

THE SKIRRID MOUNTAIN INN
The most haunted inn in Wales

THE SKIRRID MOUNTAIN INN ⚔
LLANFIHANGEL CRUCORNEY
NR ABERGAVENNY, GWENT
TEL: 01873 890258

The earliest reference to this delightful hostelry, nestling in the shadow of the Skirrid Mountain, is in AD1110 when John Crowther was sentenced to death for sheep stealing and was hanged from an interior beam. Over the subsequent 800 years, 182 felons would meet a similar fate, dangling by the neck over the building's stairwell.

An unusual style of customer relations, you may think, until you realize that as well as serving up frothing tankards to thirsty travellers, the premises also doubled as a courthouse. In the mid 19th century it pulled out of the execution business and has since dedicated itself exclusively to the sustenance of the living.

With such a sinister pedigree, The Skirrid Mountain Inn can offer many a ghostly tale to chill the blood. The spirits of those executed here often make their presences known in a rather disturbing manner. Several visitors have felt the terrifying sensation of an invisible noose being slipped around their necks and have been alarmed to feel it tighten. Although they always manage to break free from the malign grip, their necks bear the distinct impression of the rope marks for several days afterwards.

Another ghost to haunt the old and, in parts, spooky property is that of a woman who, although never seen, is felt and heard by staff as she rustles invisibly past them. As she passes, her progress is always marked by a definite chill in the air. In the 1990s, during a live radio broadcast from the inn, a medium was asked for his explanation of the encounters. He said that he sensed a young woman had died of consumption at the inn, and that she was possibly in her early thirties.

Realizing that she had no way of verifying the statement, the landlady thanked the medium politely for the information. Several months later, however, a couple researching their family tree paid the landlady a visit. They told her that they were seeking information about one of their ancestors, Harry Price, who had owned the premises during the mid 18th century. They then revealed that his wife, Fanny Price, had died of consumption in her early thirties, and was buried in the local churchyard, where she still lies today.

Opposite: Many a past customer of The Skirrid Mountain Inn ended their days dangling over its staircase back when the pub was also a courthouse.

LLINDIR INN
The salty seaman and the feckless wife

> LLINDIR INN 🛏 ✗
>
> LLINDIR STREET
> HENLLAN, DENBIGH
> TEL: 01745 812640

This 13th-century thatched inn is the haunt of a ghostly lady whom staff have come to know as Sylvia, and who in life is said to have been the wife of an 18th-century sailor who owned the inn. Frustrated by her husband's long absences at sea, the lovelorn Sylvia abandoned her marriage vows and bestowed her favours upon any local lad that took her fancy. Her husband remained blissfully unaware of his wife's infidelity until one day a favourable wind caused his ship to dock a few days sooner than anticipated. He got caught in a storm on his way home, and by the time he arrived at the inn he was drenched to the skin. He wasn't best pleased to find that his wife was not in the bar to greet him. He was even less pleased when, on stomping up the stairs to change into dry clothes, he opened the bedroom door and found her *in flagrante* with one of the local youths. Unable to contain his anger, the cuckolded husband drew his dagger, leapt onto the bed, and stabbed his rival to death. His terrified spouse sobbed for forgiveness, but he was beyond reason; moments later he had clasped her by the throat, and soon she too lay dead upon the bed.

Sylvia's ghost has remained behind ever since. It has long been held that should any man deign to spend a night alone in the room in which she died, her amorous spirit will materialize and slip into bed with him!

In November 2002 the licensee, Alan Cannon, went on holiday to the Philippines, leaving the inn in the capable hands of his son and daughter and their respective families. According to the *Vale Advertiser*, 'things got so spooky that they eventually all decided to sleep in the lounge rather than risk going to any of the bedrooms'.

Among the spectral antics that so unnerved them was a piercing shriek that echoed through the pub, and a loud buzzing noise, followed almost immediately by a door suddenly being blown open by a strong gust of wind. Alan's daughter, Sarah, was most perturbed when she returned to her room one night to find the contents of her make-up bag arranged in a semicircle on the floor.

'They were so shaken by it all,' recalled Alan, 'that they phoned me up on holiday even though it was 2.30am in Wales. They said they were terrified and wanted to leave.' Luckily he managed to reassure them that the ghosts, although alarming, were quite benign. 'I have encountered many a ghost myself at The Llindir,' Alan added by way of conclusion, 'but I have never been harmed.'

THE WEST ARMS HOTEL
The blue lady

Established in 1670, this lovely old inn, with its low ceilings, undulating slate-flagged floors, vast inglenooks and period furnishings, was once a favoured stopover for cattle drovers bringing their charges down from the tree-lined hillsides that surround it.

THE WEST ARMS HOTEL
LLANARMON, DYFFRYN CEIRIOG
LLANGOLLEN, DENBIGHSHIRE
TEL: 01691 600665

The inn is haunted by an enigmatic blue lady, whose appearances can be kept at bay by the simple device of not lighting the fire in one of the front lounges. According to tradition, the woman was killed in a fire that broke out in this room in the late 1700s. Such a sudden and unexpected exit from the world left her a little perturbed, and now whenever a fire is lit in this particular room her spirit is moved to register its displeasure. Although perfectly harmless, she has the alarming habit of drifting past bemused patrons, leaving a cold chill in her spectral wake, and then melting away into thin air. Management, therefore, have chosen to adopt a conciliatory attitude towards their resident spectre, and staff are expressly forbidden to light the fire in the lounge bar.

THE BLUE LION INN
AND CHAMBERS RESTAURANT
Murder most foul and a skeleton on the casket

Nestling amidst a maze of narrow, twisting country lanes, the tiny village of Cwm rewards the intrepid explorer with beautiful views over the Vale of Clwyd and towards the distant, brooding splendour of Snowdonia. The

THE BLUE LION INN
CWM DYSERTH, RHYL
DENBIGHSHIRE
TEL: 01745 570733

Blue Lion Inn started out as a farmhouse and acquired its resident ghost in 1646, when owned by the Henry family. One of their number, John, was killed during a heated argument with his father and brother who, to cover their tracks, buried him at a secret location and then spread the rumour that he had gone off to seek his fortune. The villagers appear to have accepted the Henrys' version of events, and soon the unfortunate John became little more than a distant memory.

In the 19th century, during renovation work in the local churchyard, a skeleton was discovered lying on top of one of the coffins. Since the remains were found outside rather than inside the casket, speculation was rife that the burial had been both hasty and illegal, and word quickly spread that the bones were those of the long-vanished John Henry.

Thereafter his spirit became a regular at the inn that now occupies his family's farmhouse. He seems to have been particularly active in the 1960s, when several landlords and landladies spoke of looking up from their duties to find his sombre revenant staring at them. After a few minutes he would turn and leave, ducking his head as he did so, as if passing under a doorway that no longer exists. On one occasion he was even seen standing in the company of his father and brother, but that appears to have been a one-off haunting and reunion that has not been repeated since.

Another ghost that haunts The Blue Lion is that of an old lady who once appeared to the young son of a previous landlord. His parents heard him chatting in his room one night, but when they went to investigate they found he was alone. When asked with whom he had been talking, he explained how a nice old woman in a blue dress had walked in and, having complained of feeling unwell, had lain down on the other bed. When the boy was shown a picture of his dead grandmother, whom he had never met, he recognized her as his mystery visitor!

THE BUSH INN
The bardic charlatan and the ghostly highwayman

> THE BUSH INN ✕
> ST HILARY, COWBRIDGE
> GLAMORGAN
> TEL: 01284 772745

This 16th-century thatched inn, with its thick walls of solid stone, low oak beams, flagstone floors, huge inglenook fireplace, spiral stone staircase and old settles and pews, is as charming and cosy an old place as you could ever wish to find. Its past customers have included the charismatic and enigmatic Iolo Morganwg who, in the mid 18th century, was responsible for the re-establishment of the Gorsedd of the Bards, a supposedly ancient druidic order, which he saw as the guardian of the Welsh language.

Although the whole thing was a fantasy and a product of Morganwg's vivid imagination, the body of bards he established certainly struck a chord with the Welsh people, giving them an association that valued their native tongue – something that hadn't existed since the Age of the Welsh Princes, hundreds of years before.

However, the man who haunts The Bush, although dating from the same age, was of a more down-to-earth nature. His name was Ianto Ffranc, a ruthless highwayman who terrorized the byways hereabouts. One day the forces of law and order caught up with him and, following a ferocious cross-country chase, the rascally robber was finally cornered in a cave, some 200 yards (180 metres) from The Bush. Following a brief exchange of pistol fire, Ffranc was captured and, having been found guilty at his subsequent trial, was executed. His ghost, however, returned to the inn he had frequented in life and close to which his career had drawn to its inglorious conclusion. Many staff and customers have encountered his phantom stomping across the main bar, a look of grim determination upon his face, as though he is setting off to carry out another heinous crime on the byways of Glamorgan.

THE GOLDEN LION
Old Jeffrey, the pensive phantom

There is a theory that buildings and articles can somehow become charged with the spirits and emotions of those who have either lived in or owned them in the past. This may well account for the unusual history behind the male ghost that haunts The Golden Lion.

| THE GOLDEN LION ✗ |
| CHESTER ROAD |
| ROSSETT, WREXHAM |
| TEL: 01244 571020 |

Known to generations of regulars as Old Jeffrey, he is said to have been a criminal who in the 17th century robbed a farm labourer near Gresford. Having subjected the unfortunate man to a savage beating, he ran off, leaving him for dead. But the man recovered and was able to identify his assailant, and Jeffrey paid for his crime by being hanged. After his execution, his body was brought to Rossett and gibbeted on the village green. It hung there for some time, a gruesome warning to others who might contemplate similar evil.

The locals, however, came to fear the rotting cadaver, and eventually a group of them tore down the gibbet and buried Jeffrey on the green. The gibbet was broken up and one palette of its wood was incorporated into an outbuilding of The Golden Lion, where it survives today. With it came the spirit of 'Old Jeffrey', and he has remained at the inn ever since.

On the whole, his is a harmless ghost that tends to be more mischievous than malicious. Items get moved around behind the bar, and glasses have been known to swing on their pegs as if an invisible presence has run a finger along them. Very occasionally his apparition will materialize before witnesses for a few chilling minutes, staring pensively into space, before melting away into thin air.

THE CASTLE HOTEL
The maid who saw the future

> THE CASTLE HOTEL ⊨ ✕
> HIGH STREET
> CONWY, CONWY
> TEL: 01492 582800

The elegant Castle Hotel stands on the site of a Cistercian abbey, and at one stage consisted of two hostelries, the 15th-century Kings Head and The Castle. Since the latter was the larger of the two, it was only fair that, when they were combined into one establishment, it should assume its name. In its time it has played host to the likes of the great Victorian engineer, Thomas Telford, the poet William Wordsworth, and even the Queen of Romania, who dropped by for lunch during her visit to nearby Llandudno in 1890.

Several ghosts are said to haunt The Caslte. The most famous is that of a former chambermaid who in life possessed the uncanny ability for predicting the future. So accurate were her prophecies that people would travel from far and wide to have their fortunes told. One day, however, the chambermaid vividly foresaw her own death. So convinced was she by the chilling premonition that she made the landlord promise to send her body back to her native Anglesey for burial when the time came. Shortly afterwards, she was taken ill and did indeed die. The landlord, who had not for a moment believed he would have to make good his promise, decided against sending her corpse back to Anglesey and had her laid to rest in the local graveyard.

This blatant disregard for her wishes stirred the maid's spirit to indignation, and she made her displeasure known by subjecting The Castle to a severe bout of poltergeist activity. Food would be lifted from the tables and flung across the room in front of bemused customers. Beer barrels would be mysteriously emptied, and wine bottles would suddenly explode for no apparent reason. Waiters would be tripped up with the result that meals would end up in the laps of astonished, not to say, furious patrons. Horses would be set free to run amok and cause mayhem on Conwy High Street. And the maid's ghost appeared before the landlord one night, dragged him from his bed and spirited him high into the air above the inn, where she threatened to drop him. Needless to say, the landlord was forced to concede defeat, and the chamber-maid's cadaver was exhumed and reburied on her native Anglesey.

Although this curbed her more extreme activity, it by no means drove her spirit from the inn. She has been seen many times walking along Conwy High Street, dressed in old-fashioned garb and wearing a black coat. Witnesses don't realize she is a ghost until she turns abruptly towards The

Castle Hotel and disappears into one of its solid walls. Interestingly, there used to be a door at the spot where she now vanishes, although it has long since been bricked up.

THE RHOS FYNACH
PUB AND RESTAURANT
The thieving phantom

Although resident ghosts rarely prove frightening, their antics can nonetheless be both irritating and inconvenient. Small objects can disappear for days on end

THE RHOS FYNACH PUB AND RESTAURANT ✗
RHOS PROMENADE, RHOS-ON-SEA
COLWYN BAY, CONWY
TEL: 01492 548185

and then turn up in the most unlikely places. However, in December 2002 Robert Skelley, owner of the historic Rhos Fynach Pub, was confronted with a possible spectral conundrum that baffled even the case-hardened officers of the North Wales Constabulary.

On Tuesday 3 December, staff discovered that the Christmas tree, which they had painstakingly decorated just a few days before, had disappeared overnight. According to the *North Wales Weekly News*, Robert and his staff were 'mortified to learn that someone – or something – had stolen their 5-foot fake fir, along with the £40 worth of baubles, tinsel and ribbon which adorned it'.

Mystified as to how the tree could have been smuggled from the pub without them noticing, staff reported the theft to the North Wales police. Officers from Special Branch began an investigation into whether 'the offender (or even the tree) [had been] caught on CCTV in the streets of Rhos-on-Sea'. But when this line of investigation failed to root out the perpetrators, staff began mooting the chilling possibility that the pub's 12th-century spectre may have taken the tree as a festive prank.

'We do have the ghost of a monk,' Robert explained, 'as it's a very old building and, given the sudden disappearance ... he has to be considered a suspect.'

The mystery took on an added twist when, on the morning after the *North Wales Weekly News* had reported the crime, the Christmas tree – complete with baubles, tinsel and ribbon – was found standing in the pub's delivery entrance. Tied to one of its branches was a note that read, 'Thanks for bringing the Christmas spirit to those who need it most. Next year I'll ask. Yours truly. The Rhos Fynach Ghost.'

THE GRAPES HOTEL
She'll scare you plumb rigid

Although the cellars may well date back to the 13th century, most of The Grapes Hotel was built in the 17th century. It is a delightfully cosy and unpretentious pub, nestling within the shadow of Snowdon. George Borrow, author of *Wild Wales*, was

THE GRAPES HOTEL ⇔ ✗
MAENTWROG
BLANEAN FFESTINIOG, GWYNNEDD
TEL: 01766 590208

once a visitor, and he applauded its 'magnificent parlour', where he partook of brandy and water. Later, Lloyd George dropped in, as did Lillie Langtry.

The Grapes is haunted by the mysterious figure of a little old lady in Victorian clothing who has a propensity for shocking the staff in the downstairs bar. One minute staff will be alone in the bar, the next they will turn to find her gazing at them intensely. They have no time to register either shock or fear before she vanishes as quickly and mysteriously as she appeared. Her identity is unknown, and since she confines her ghostly activity to these brief encounters, she is welcome to remain until such time as she tires of, as the management put it, frightening the kitchen staff 'plumb rigid'!

THE SUN INN
The ghostly mother and child

Nestling at the heart of the pretty village of St Florence, near Tenby, the 17th-century Sun Inn, furnished with unusual bits and pieces such as an old butcher's block that serves as a bar table, is a lovely, cosy village pub. Since the old inn stands right next to the graveyard,

THE SUN INN ✗
ST FLORENCE, NR TENBY
DYFED, PEMBROKESHIRE
TEL: 01834 871322

it is inevitable that it should have a ghost or two milling about.

The ghosts in question are those of a mother holding a small baby. Who they were is not known, but some long-forgotten tragedy seems to have left their spirits earthbound, two sad shades that glide around the bar area, oblivious to those whose paths they cross. There is nothing at all frightening about them, and witnesses claim to find their overall bearing sad rather than scary. Having enjoyed a few moments of spectral investigation the two will slowly fade away until nothing but a cold chill remains as testimony to their visit.

Opposite: Visitors to The Grapes Hotel may well encounter an elderly Victorian lady who might scare them 'plumb rigid'!

SCOTLAND

DUMFRIES & GALLOWAY, BORDERS, MIDLOTHIAN, ARGYLL, PERTH & KINROSS, ABERDEENSHIRE, FIFE, STIRLING & HIGHLAND

The Stair Arms Hotel, Pathhead, Midlothian – see page 145
*The ghost of an old maid is regularly seen gliding up and down
the main staircase.*

The majority of Scottish inns date from the era of the stagecoach, when the opening of new routes led to an increase in travel. To accommodate this new clientele a plethora of wayside hostelries sprung up, many of them resulting from a Government-sponsored inn-building initiative unique to Scotland. Lairds, too, got in on the act and built inns on their estates, the size and grandeur of which were often intended to advertise their personal wealth and status. As a consequence, Scotland offers a vast selection of old inns, and the ghosts that wander them are, to say the least, intriguing. From the ghost of Robert Burns's mistress at The Globe Inn in Dumfries, to the poignant shade of the shivering Blue Boy who haunts The Coylett Inn on the tranquil shores of Loch Eck, they are a varied bunch whose stories often touch upon the lives of famous Scottish figures.

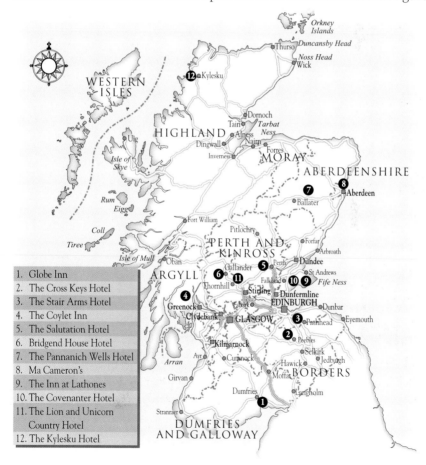

1. Globe Inn
2. The Cross Keys Hotel
3. The Stair Arms Hotel
4. The Coylet Inn
5. The Salutation Hotel
6. Bridgend House Hotel
7. The Pannanich Wells Hotel
8. Ma Cameron's
9. The Inn at Lathones
10. The Covenanter Hotel
11. The Lion and Unicorn Country Hotel
12. The Kylesku Hotel

GLOBE INN
Robert Burns and the lovely ghost

GLOBE INN 🛏 ✕
56 HIGH STREET
DUMFRIES, DUMFRIES & GALLOWAY
TEL: 01387 252335

As you stroll along Dumfries High Street you may notice a sign protruding from an overhead wall, bearing a portrait of Scotland's national poet, Robert Burns. Beneath it a narrow, sinister alleyway leads the curious explorer to a snug little time capsule, which a large beam, spanning the width of the passage, announces as The Globe Inn, one of Scotland's most historic and atmospheric hostelries. The pub's interior – with its labyrinth of cosy rooms, hidden nooks and dark corners – is a veritable shrine to Robert Burns. There is hardly an inch of wall that does not display a piece of memorabilia to the man who, just three months before his death, described The Globe as having been 'for many years my Howff [haunt]', where he had enjoyed 'many a merry squeeze'. Even two of the window-panes bear lines etched by the Bard himself, using his diamond ring.

One of the inn's attractions for Burns was barmaid Anna Park, a niece of the then landlord and landlady, William 'Jock' Hyslop and his wife, Meg. The close friendship between Burns and Anna developed into an affair that inspired what Burns regarded as one of his best love songs, in which he eulogized her:

Yest're'en I had a pint of wine,
A place where body saw na;
Yest're'en lay on this breast o'mine,
The gowden locks o' Anna.

But their affair ended in tragedy when Anna died, shortly after giving birth to an illegitimate daughter. Burns never denied that he was the father of the child, and his wife, Jean, raised the little girl as one of her own family. Today, the bedroom that Robert Burns used when lodging at The Globe, and in which he is said to have conducted his trysts with Anna, is once more used to accommodate paying guests.

But you do not have to stay the night in order to make the acquaintance of the benevolent female spirit that haunts the inn. Indeed, you are just as likely

Opposite: The lauded Scottish poet Robert Burns called the Globe his favourite haunt, but it is his mistress, Anna Park, who roams the pub during twilight hours in spirit form.

to encounter her when the bar is lively and busy. The fact that she is dressed in the attire of an 18th-century maidservant has even led some to wonder if she might not be the ghost of Anna Park herself. She is known to appear whenever change occurs at the inn, or when the rafters ring to the sound of celebration. It would, of course, be nice if she could be reunited with the ghost of Robert Burns. But that is unlikely, as it is his literary rather than literal spirit with which this special hostelry is imbued.

THE CROSS KEYS HOTEL
Marion Ritchie, the ghostly hostess

THE CROSS KEYS HOTEL 🛏 ✗
24 NORTHGATE
PEEBLES, BORDERS
TEL: 01721 724222

The Cross Keys, formerly known as The Yett, is the oldest inn in Peebles. Built in 1693, as the town house of the Williamsons, it became an inn in the early 18th century. By 1769 it was being run by the Ritchie family, one of whom, Marion Ritchie, would become indelibly linked with the building.

Marion is said to have ruled over her hostelry with a rod of despotic iron. Customers who had the audacity to over-imbibe would have their drinks snatched from their grasp by their hostess and be told in no uncertain terms to 'Gang hame tae yer wife and bairns'. Such was her repute that Sir Walter Scott, a frequenter of The Cross Keys, used her as his prototype for Meg Dods, the landlady of 'detestable bad humour' whose 'kitchen was her pride and joy', in his novel *St Ronan's Well*.

Marion Ritchie died on 8 February 1822, reputedly in bedroom 5 of the hotel. But such was the level of her dedication to her inn that her spirit has remained behind at the old pub to keep a keen eye on the daily comings and goings. Sometimes she simply moves things around. At other times she will slam doors, or bang and clatter around in rooms that are known to be empty.

Modern labour-saving devices are particularly irksome to the lady who, in life, ruled her servants with a heavy hand. All types of electrical equipment have been known to switch off of their own accord, and at the most inopportune moments. On several occasions, however, Marion's revenant has been known to manifest itself as a full apparition, gliding about her premises and no doubt ensuring that today's staff and customers adhere to the strict standards of service and behaviour that the inn's oldest resident demands. And so she keeps her spectral watch a trapped memory lingering on in the place that was once her fiefdom.

THE STAIR ARMS HOTEL
The ghostly suicide

The Stair Arms was built in the 1830s by
Lord and Lady Stair, and originally catered
for travellers whom Thomas Telford's
nearby Lothian Bridge brought clattering
along the dusty Great North Road (now the

THE STAIR ARMS HOTEL ⚒
PATHHEAD, MIDLOTHIAN
TEL: 01875 320277

busy A68) in ever-increasing numbers. By the early 20th century it had become
one of Scotland's many temperance hotels and later, as horse-drawn transport
gave way to the petrol engine, it expanded to meet the needs of the more
discerning modern traveller.

Such is the standard of its hospitality that several past residents show
a marked reluctance to depart, and have opted instead to remain within its
warm sandstone walls as spirits. The ghost of an 'old maid' is regularly seen
gliding up and down the main staircase, while a spectral 'green lady' keeps to a
time-worn route between rooms 1 and 8. The hotel's back corridor, meanwhile,
occasionally resonates to poltergeist activity as some unseen entity moves
things round in a fit of phantom pique. There is a tradition that the spirit
responsible is that of an early 20th-century manager who, following a love affair
that went awry, attempted to commit suicide by slashing his wrists. When this
failed, he made his way to the Lothian Bridge and threw himself off.

THE COYLET INN
The Blue Boy's poignant spectre

The brooding, pine-clad hills that
surround this 17th-century coaching inn
cast long shadows over its whitewashed
walls, creating an air of enchantment. It
overlooks the dark, choppy waters of

THE COYLET INN ⚒
LOCH ECK, ARGYLL
TEL: 01369 840426

Loch Eck – the name of which is thought to derive from the Gaelic *each*,
meaning horse. This probably refers to the legendary water-horses or kelpies
that were once thought to reside in the murky depths of freshwater lochs.

Loch Eck certainly provides a tranquil setting for The Coylet Inn, but its
proximity once resulted in a tragedy that has resulted in a childish shade
roaming the pub's cosy interior. This ghostly child's living self, whose name
has long since been forgotten, was in the habit of sleepwalking. One night,
while staying at the inn, he embarked upon a nocturnal wander that ended
abruptly when he plunged into the freezing waters of the loch. When his body

was recovered the next morning, his flesh was blue with cold. Ever since, the 'Blue Boy's' phantom has made periodic returns to the old inn, desperately searching for his mother. Sometimes he appears as a full-blown apparition, at other times he simply indulges in the annoying practice of moving items around. But perhaps his most chilling habit is that of walking unseen through the building and leaving wet footprints in his ghostly wake.

THE SALUTATION HOTEL
Bonnie Prince Charlie rides again

THE SALUTATION HOTEL 🛏✕
34 SOUTH STREET
PERTH, PERTH & KINROSS
TEL: 01738 630066

The Salutation Inn has been welcoming guests through its doors since 1699. The present building, more elegant hotel than snug coaching inn, has been added to over the centuries in a piecemeal fashion that has produced a cornucopia of architectural styles. The façade was designed by the King's Architect for Scotland, Robert Reid, and dates from the early 19th century, by which time the 'Sally' – as it is known locally – had acquired its most illustrious ghost, Charles Stuart, Bonnie Prince Charlie. Perth was the first Scottish town to fall to his forces during his 1745 campaign to regain the British throne for the Stuarts. Indeed, the hotel's name is said to date from this period when the proprietor, John Burt, enthusiastically shook the Prince's hand in salutation. It is said that Bonnie Prince Charlie did not actually sleep at the inn, but used a room here to hold meetings with his commanders. His ghost, resplendent in green tartan, has reputedly been seen in the chamber he occupied, now renamed the Stuart Room in his honour. Whether his was the kilted figure that once startled a woman guest, who found him standing by her bed in the middle of one night in the 1970s, has never been established – no sooner had she recovered from the shock than the spectral visitor vanished.

The site on which the hotel stands was once part of the Franciscan (Greyfriars) monastery. Periodic refurbishments of the building have uncovered ancient fire-scarred walls behind more recent plasterwork, leading to speculation that an older building here may have been destroyed by fire. This may account for the ghostly monk whose shimmering shade has been known to chill the blood of staff working in the hotel's former ballroom, now used as the breakfast room. He is more tantalizing enigma than terrifying entity, and witnesses only ever catch brief glimpses as he drifts silently by, intent on some ethereal, though unknown, monastic task.

BRIDGEND HOUSE HOTEL
The ghost's footpath

Callander is a delightful resort, nestling amidst the splendour of The Trossachs. It rose to prominence when Sir Walter Scott's poem *The Lady of the Lake* (inspired by nearby Loch Katrine) sparked off an invasion of Victorian

BRIDGEND HOUSE HOTEL 🛏 ✗
BRIDGEND
CALLANDER, PERTH & KINROSS
TEL: 01877 330130

tourists, flocking to explore the wild and untamed landscapes about which Scott waxed so lyrically. In the 1960s it became well known to television viewers as 'Tannochbrae' in the series *Dr Finlay's Casebook*. It remains a popular tourist destination, and such is the purity of its air that in 1997 Michael Jackson was even rumoured to be house hunting in the neighbourhood *sans* mask!

The annual influx of visitors is well served by a plethora of hotels and inns. One of the snuggest and most atmospheric is the Bridgend House Hotel, a 17th-century coaching inn whose black-and-white timbered exterior seems strangely at odds with the other buildings nearby. This mock Tudor appearance results from renovation work carried out after an RAF pilot literally 'dropped in' when his spitfire crashed into the hotel's car park during World War II.

As one of the oldest hostelries in Callander, the building has had ample opportunity to acquire a ghost or two. Part of the inn was reputedly built over a footpath, which once led to the meadow behind. This may explain the occasional phantom forms that have been known to suddenly materialize from walls to simply disappear into the one opposite. Employees, sleeping alone on the premises in the winter months, are sometimes awoken by footsteps clattering across the floors in the early hours, and have also been disturbed by the sound of doors opening and closing.

THE PANNANICH WELLS HOTEL
Queen Victoria slept here!

Around 1760 a terminally ill woman dreamt that if she were to bathe in the spring that bubbled from the slopes of Pannanich Hill she would be cured. Summoning up all her strength, she struggled to the hillside

THE PANNANICH WELLS HOTEL 🛏 ✗
SOUTH DEESIDE ROAD
NR BALLATER, ABERDEENSHIRE
TEL: 01339 755018

and plunged headlong into the pool whereupon, sure enough, her health was miraculously restored. Soon afterwards an entrepreneurial local laird capped the spring and went into the spa business. As the fame of the Pannanich Wells began to spread, he built a small hotel to accommodate those who came to take the curative waters. Lord Byron paid a visit in 1795, as did Sir Walter Scott in 1822. Later Queen Victoria was an honoured guest and applauded the 'humble but very clean accommodation' of the 'curios little old inn'.

Today that same hostelry still stands at the foot of the picturesque slope of Pannanich Hill, and affords stunning views over the tranquil beauty of the Dee Valley. Its granite walls belie a snug interior, where the ghost of an elegant young woman dressed in a grey blouse and long, grey skirt makes occasional appearances. It is thought to be her restless wraith that is sometimes heard moving furniture around inside empty rooms, or which invisibly opens and closes doors. Hers may also be the delicate scent that from time to time wafts around room 1 of the hotel. Her spectral antics have come to be an accepted fixture and, since she is a harmless spectre, those who have chanced upon her have come to regard her with affection rather than fear, and are content to let her be.

MA CAMERON'S
Knock knock, who's there?

MA CAMERON'S ✕
6 LITTLE BELMONT STREET
ABERDEEN, ABERDEENSHIRE
TEL: 01224 644487

A popular hangout with students from Aberdeen University, this bustling and vibrant city-centre pub began life as Cameron's Inn, and was founded by Charles Ingram in the late 18th century. Over the years it evolved into a popular coaching inn, its solid granite walls affording shelter and sustenance to thousands of weary travellers. In the 1930s it came into the possession of one Elizabeth Mitchell. It has been alleged that she was 'Ma Cameron', by which name subsequent generations of tipplers came to know the old hostelry. Although this claim is disputed, the appellation has stuck, and is now the official name of the inn.

Although a recent refurbishment has greatly expanded the pub, a delightful snug bar survives to the right of the main entrance, and here you can while away a peaceful hour or two, enjoying a wee dram while admiring the prints of old Aberdeen that adorn the walls. It is also worth keeping a keen ear cocked for the ghostly sounds that have been known to echo from sundry parts of the old building. The first sure sign that something ethereal is afoot is a sudden drop in temperature. This can be followed by various strange occurrences – footsteps plodding their weary way across rooms that are known to be empty, or an unseen presence brushing by.

On one occasion a decorator was painting the ceiling in the lounge bar when three loud knocks sounded from the room overhead. Since he knew for certain that he was the only person in the building, he reciprocated by rapping hard upon the ceiling only to hear someone, or something, return the knocking. Soon, however, his unseen companion grew tired of this spectral game of 'knock, knock' and allowed him to finish the ceiling without further disturbance.

THE INN AT LATHONES
Love among the dunes

This charming 400-year-old roadside coaching inn enjoys an isolated setting amidst remote and beautiful countryside. It has a plain white exterior that belies a snug, cosy interior where a warm welcome awaits. Much of that

> THE INN AT LATHONES ⌣ ✗
> LATHONES, BY LARGOWARD
> LEVEN, FIFE
> TEL: 01334 840494

warmth emanates from the fireplace, above which is a traditional wedding stone commemorating the marriage of Iona Kirk to Ewan Lindsay in 1718. Having plighted their troth, the couple settled down to run the inn together. Such was the depth of their love that when Iona died in 1736 the wedding stone is said to have cracked, and shortly thereafter Ewan also died, possibly of a broken heart. It has been suggested that Iona may be the ghostly grey lady who is now the inn's best-known phantom, and whose harmless shade is content to lead a spectral horse in and out of what were once the stables, but which have now been converted into a bar.

Later in the 18th century, the remote countryside hereabouts was the hunting ground of a notorious highwayman whose short stature (he was less than 5 feet/1.5 metres tall) led to his being nicknamed 'Wee Mad MacGregor'. Many was the time that, having relieved saddle-sore wayfarers of their burdensome possessions, he would drop into the inn to slake his thirst and spend some of his ill-gotten gains on a hearty meal. The fact that he was hideously disfigured on one side of his body, so that his face drooped alarmingly, causing him to drool uncontrollably from the corner of his mouth, allowed him to dine without fear of interruption.

Today the property has settled into old age and basks in the distinction of being St Andrew's oldest coaching inn. The grey lady aside, other strange phenomena have been known to occur within its weathered walls. There was the time when a group of German guests, enjoying a talk on whisky in the

stable bar, had the audacity to cast doubt upon the veracity of the inn's ghostly reputation. They changed their minds when the fireplace tools were suddenly lifted up by an unseen hand and moved to the other side of the hearth!

Occasionally the night-time stillness is shattered by the disturbing sound of a crying baby that echoes from the upstairs rooms, now used as offices. Several guests have also awoken from a deep sleep to find a mysterious white mist swirling over their heads. But far from being frightened by the experience, they describe its effect as calming and refreshing.

THE COVENANTER HOTEL
The ghostly covenanter

Falkland, with its picturesque old houses and cobbled streets, sits at the foot of the Lomond Hills and is one of the loveliest towns in Scotland. The graceful and beautiful Falkland Palace, once a favoured residence of Scottish Kings,

THE COVENANTER HOTEL
HIGH STREET, FALKLAND
CUPAR, FIFE
TEL: 01337 857224

soars majestically over its main street. It was here on 14 December 1542 that James V, hoping for a son, learnt that his wife, Marie of Guise, had given birth to a daughter, the future Mary, Queen of Scots. With a sigh of weary resignation James turned his face to the wall and died.

A little way past the palace stands a small inn that almost cowers beneath the shadows of its loftier neighbours. It dates largely from the 18th century, although parts might be much older. It is called The Covenanter Hotel, and is named for the fact that Richard Cameron, the 'Lion of the Covenanters', was born a few houses along.

In early adulthood, Cameron worked as a schoolmaster in Falkland, and also served in the Episcopalian church. In 1672, however, he was converted to the Covenanter cause and became a vociferous opponent of Charles II's attempts to force Episcopalian worship on Scotland. Cameron's skill and eloquence as an orator ensured a dedicated following. In 1680 he was instrumental in drawing up the Sanquhar Declaration, which not only rejected Charles II's authority, but also declared war on him. Accused of treason, a reward of 5,000 marks was offered for Cameron's capture, and English soldiers were sent to scour the Scottish countryside for him.

Opposite: Almost dwarfed by its loftier neighbours, Falkland's Covenanter Hotel commemorates the town's famous son, Richard Cameron.

On the morning of 22 July 1680, Cameron, having just finished washing, suddenly held his hands high and cried out, 'This is the last washing. I have need to make them clean for there are many to see them'. That day a group of English dragoons finally caught up with his small band of 63 loyal followers on the moor at Ayrsmoss in Ayrshire. Deciding to stand and fight, Cameron was heard to pray, 'Lord, spare the green, and take the ripe'. The English soldiers had little trouble overpowering his supporters and Richard Cameron was killed. His head and hands were cut off and carried in a basket to Edinburgh, where they were cruelly shown to his father, languishing in prison for Covenanting activities. After that they were placed on public display and, just as Cameron had prophesied, were seen by many people.

However, Richard Cameron's is not the ghost that wanders the hotel now named in his honour. A female phantom roams the wonderfully atmospheric stairway and corridors of The Covenanter Hotel. Some claim that she is the ghost of Mary Queen of Scots, who spent some of her happiest times at the nearby palace. Her appearances are always presaged by a sudden drop in temperature and accompanied by the delicate scent of lavender, left hanging in the air as she glides gracefully past those upon whom she bestows the honour of her ghostly companionship.

THE LION AND UNICORN COUNTRY HOTEL
Elizabeth Taylor and the ghostly lady

THE LION AND UNICORN COUNTRY HOTEL 🛏️✕
MAIN STREET
THORNHILL, STIRLING
TEL: 01786 850204

With its interior walls of exposed rough stone, low ceilings of hand-hewn timber and coal fire blazing away in an enormous fireplace, The Lion and Unicorn is as snug a hostelry as you could ever wish to encounter. Established in 1635 as a drovers' inn, it has been attending to the needs of parched and hungry travellers ever since. Visitors today can spot a blocked niche in one of the walls, which was once the hatch through which food and drink were passed out to the drovers.

The inn was also a notorious haunt of cattle thieves and rustlers. Rob Roy MacGregor is said to have paid the tavern a visit and, more recently, the warning to 'Beware of the Regulars' above the public bar entrance did not deter Billy Connolly from popping in. Actress Elizabeth Taylor found the allure of its pretty whitewashed exterior irresistible when driving past one evening in 1980. She stopped for a bite to eat and was so pleased with the hospitality that she decided to stay the night. Staff and regulars still speak fondly of the day when Hollywood came to Thornhill.

The inn is reputedly haunted by a harmless female entity who wears a green flowing dress, whom staff and regulars have nicknamed Annie. Some claim that she is the spirit of a former resident who, possibly following a disastrous love affair, flung herself to her death from an upstairs window. Whatever the cause of her demise, Annie seems content to glide aimlessly about the lower levels of the premises, bothering no one and leaving a feeling of happiness and well-being in her wake.

A phantom male companion of Annie's was responsible for giving a chef a nasty shock one morning. The chef was in the pub's garden when he happened to glance up to find the upper half of a man floating in mid-air before him. Moments later the truncated ghostly visitor disappeared and has never graced the inn with a visit, legless or otherwise, since.

THE KYLESKU HOTEL

Whisky galore

A long time ago a fisherman wandering along the shores of Loch a Chairn Bhain noticed a barrel of whisky bobbing up and down on its choppy waters. Dragging it ashore, he manhandled it to the nearest inn, The Ferryhouse (as The Kylesku

THE KYLESKU HOTEL 🛏 ✕
KYLESKU, BY LAIRG
SOUTHERLAND, HIGHLAND
TEL: 01971 502231

Hotel was then called). The name at that time derived from the ferry that departed from the landing stage outside the inn, and which transported traffic over the loch before the Kylesku Bridge rendered it redundant. The fisherman placed his find in the attic of the inn and that night invited his friends to join him in a rowdy celebration of his good fortune.

As the evening wore on and the whisky flowed freely, the fisherman's son became worried about the approaching Sabbath and attempted to persuade his father to call a halt to the drunken festivities. His father would not listen, and gave his son a drunken shove. The son retaliated, and a fight ensued, resulting in the father taking a fatal tumble down the outside stairs that led from the attic. With his dying breath the wounded father slurred a curse upon his offspring.

Not long after, the son drowned in the loch, and ever since the ghost of the fisherman is said to appear at the inn on the anniversary of his death – although when that is, only the walls of the old inn know, and they're not telling!

IRELAND

COUNTY DOWN, COUNTY ANTRIM, COUNTY GALWAY, COUNTY CLARE, COUNTY TIPPERARY, COUNTY KILKENNY & COUNTY DUBLIN

Renvyle House Hotel, Renvyle, Connemara, County Galway – see page 158

As Mrs Yeats stood by the fireside, a vapoury mist appeared, which gradually assumed the form of a red-haired, pale-faced boy aged around fourteen.

The inns of Ireland proved to be something of a surprise as there were very few written accounts of pub hauntings here. Whereas in England a haunted pub is often seen as a bonus for attracting custom, in Ireland ghosts belong to a hidden realm, not to be openly advertised or spoken about for fear of driving custom away. That said, I did find some lovely old pubs and historic wayside inns. My fondest memory is of O'Brien's Bar in Churchtown, County Cork. It was Oliver Reed's local and he is buried in the graveyard opposite. I had read that several locals had seen his ghost waving to them from the burial ground when they left the bar at night. I plucked up the courage to ask about the veracity of this story, but it transpired, it was – to quote the landlord – 'a crock'. But at least I had the pleasure of meeting the man who honours Oliver Reed's memory by pouring a pint of Guinness over his grave at closing time!

GRACE NEILL'S
Where John Keats felt unwelcome

GRACE NEILL'S ✕
33 HIGH STREET
DONAGHADEE, COUNTY DOWN
TEL: 028 9188 2553

Grace Neill's claims the distinction of being the oldest pub in Ireland. It first opened its doors for business in 1611 and was originally called The Kings Arms. When the poet John Keats visited Donaghadee on a 'beautiful sunny day' he was most impressed with how 'charming and clean' the town was. The inhabitants, on the other hand, struck him as a 'rough and savage' bunch, especially the regulars at The Kings Arms, where he was 'treated to ridicule, scorn and violent abuse by the local people [who] objected to my mode of dress and thought I was some strange foreigner' which, given that he was from England, was probably a fair supposition!

Grace Neill, who died at the age of 98, ran the inn for much of the 19th and early 20th centuries. She was a characterful lady who kept a commodious establishment and liked to keep a watchful eye on proceedings while enjoying an indulgent puff on her clay pipe. Quite what Keats would have made of her custom of greeting strangers to her inn with a welcoming kiss is anybody's guess!

Although Grace died in 1916, her guiding spirit remained behind to ensure that the hostelry that now bears her name continued to operate with the smooth efficiency her clients had come to expect. Several portraits of her gaze down from the walls, and the dark, cosy front bar, with its delightful little snuggery – said to have been constructed from old ships' timbers – can have changed little since her tenure. It is here, away from the much larger and newer back rooms, where the pub's ghostly activity occurs. Members of staff have looked on in astonishment as an unseen hand has moved glasses and books around. Lights get switched on and off. Slow, ponderous footsteps have been heard crossing the upstairs floors, chilling the blood of many a tippler in the bar below. Occasionally there are reported sightings of a Victorian lady, described as being 'contained within a puff of steam', flitting about the darker recesses of the premises, and people have felt an invisible presence 'pass through them' in the vicinity of the pub's staircase.

But the management are at pains to point out that customers have nothing to fear from Grace, and describe her as a friendly and welcome wraith. And since the list of past customers is as diverse as Peter the Great of Russia, the composer Franz Liszt, former Beirut hostage Brian Keenan and pop diva Tina Turner, it's comforting to know that Grace's guiding spirit is still around to ensure that the staff adhere to the standards of hospitality she insisted upon – although a welcoming kiss (unless the circumstances are exceptional!) is no longer on offer.

DOBBINS INN HOTEL
The sad shade of Maude

Around AD1200 Reginald D'Aubin was granted a parcel of land in the shadow of Carrickfergus Castle. He set about building a tower house, which remained in the possession of his descendents for hundreds of years. By the 15th century,

DOBBINS INN HOTEL ⊭ ✕
6–8 HIGH STREET
CARRICKFERGUS, COUNTY ANTRIM
TEL: 028 9335 1905

the family name had been changed to Dobyn and successive generations became important local dignitaries, several holding high civic office. In the reign of King James I, during the Plantation of Ulster, their house became a shelter for Catholic priests who would celebrate secret masses on the premises, and a 'priest's hole', dating from these troubled times, is still visible in the hotel's reception.

It was during this period that the inn acquired its resident ghost. Elizabeth, wife of the owner, Hugh Dobbins, fell in love with a handsome soldier stationed at the castle. At night she would creep through a secret tunnel (the entrance to which is still evident at the back of the fireplace in the reception) to meet her soldier love, remembered simply as 'Buttoncap'. But her husband discovered their affair and, according to contemporary accounts, 'did put them to death with his sword'. It's not recorded whether or not Hugh Dobbins was punished, but Elizabeth's ghost has wandered the building ever since.

In 1946 the old property was converted into a hotel and the spirit of Elizabeth – or Maude, as she for some reason became known – lingered on. Several guests have been wakened from their slumbers by the light touch of a ghostly hand caressing their faces. Others have caught glimpses of a furtive figure flitting across the reception and disappearing into the stone fireplace. A waiter working in the restaurant one night was struck on the back of the leg by a coin, but when he turned around, found that the room was empty.

BALLYGALLY CASTLE HOTEL
The ghostly prankster and the distraught infant

Part 17th-century castle, part modern hotel, Ballygally Castle is surrounded by brooding hills and gazes out over the grey waters of the Irish Sea. A winding staircase twists its way up the inner wall of the castle to the sparsely furnished

BALLYGALLY CASTLE HOTEL ⊭ ✕
274 COAST ROAD, BALLYGALLY
LARNE, COUNTY ANTRIM
TEL: 028 2858 3212

'ghost room'. It has a melancholic air, complemented by the portrait of a sad-looking lady that gazes down from one of the room's whitewashed walls. Her name was Lady Isabella Shaw, and hers is the revenant that roams this imposing fortress. Tradition holds that her husband longed for a son, but when his wife gave birth to a daughter his anger knew no bounds. He imprisoned them both in this, the highest room of the castle, and left them to starve. Heartbroken by the cruelty of her spouse, the distraught lady took her baby in her arms, opened the window and leapt to her death.

Lady Isabella's ghost is now said to walk a time-worn path around the sturdy bastion and has a particular fondness for knocking loudly on guests' doors. Yet when they answer there is never anyone there. Annoying as this spectral prank might be, it pales in comparison to the more disturbing phenomena that occurs in the vicinity of the ghost room. Several people ascending the old staircase have heard the sounds of a baby sobbing. As they hurry to comfort the anguished infant, its bawling grows louder and becomes more distraught. But when they reach the apparent source of the noise, and push open the door of the ghost room, the cries suddenly cease and they find that the room is empty.

RENVYLE HOUSE HOTEL
W.B. Yeats, the ghost raiser

RENVYLE HOUSE HOTEL 🛏 ✕
RENVYLE, CONNEMARA
COUNTY GALWAY
TEL: 035 3954 3511

Renvyle House sits in quiet seclusion amidst the wilds of Connemara, and is as far off the beaten track as you could wish to be. A long, low grey-stone building standing hard by the waters of the Atlantic, it was rebuilt in the 1930s following the destruction of the former property on the site by the IRA. Never is its location so exposed, its impact so dramatic, as when a murderous gale comes howling across the ocean's raging surface and hurls itself with demented fury at walls and windows. These are the days to huddle close to the glowing turf fires, and speak in reverential whispers of the ghosts that roam the sea-sprayed house.

The current building opened on 26 April 1930 and was then owned by Dublin surgeon, poet and wit, Oliver St John Gogarty. He had purchased the original property in 1917, and unwittingly acquired several ghosts along with the deeds. There was a north-facing upstairs room, with heavy bars across its windows, where no maidservant would dare sleep for fear of the 'presence' that could be felt there. One night the malevolent force moved a heavy linen chest across the door, barring outside access. Only when a workman had sawed through the bars could the family enter the room again. One night

Gogarty was sleeping in the west wing when he was woken by ponderous, limping footsteps approaching along the corridor. Lighting a candle, he went to investigate, but the moment he left his room the flame was extinguished and he found himself alone in the dark. Suddenly his limbs became very heavy, 'as if I were exercising with rubber ropes,' as he later put it. Fortunately, nothing further happened that night.

One of St John Gogarty's closest friends was the poet W.B. Yeats. When he and his wife, Georgia, came to stay the supernatural activity increased dramatically. One night, as he sat with his companions in the oak-panelled library, the door suddenly creaked wide open. The other occupants were terrified, but Yeats raised his hand and shouted, 'Leave it alone, it will go away, as it came,' whereupon the invisible revenant obligingly slammed the door shut.

Evan Morgan (later Lord Tredgar) was less in command of the spirits. He had recently embraced Roman Catholicism, and on being told that a particular room was haunted, attempted an exorcism. No sooner had he lit three candles and began reciting some prayers than a thick mist filled the room and the unfortunate Morgan was thrown to the ground. Having been dragged to safety by his friends, he revealed that he had seen the ghost of a pale-faced boy with large luminous eyes, dressed in brown, who was clasping his hands to his throat as if strangling himself. Morgan concluded that the boy had committed suicide in that room.

W.B. Yeats, meanwhile, held a séance in an attempt to contact the ghost. Using automatic writing the spirit indicated that it objected to the presence of strangers in the house. It informed Yeats that it would appear to his wife and reveal its identity. Georgia Yeats was a well-known and talented medium and felt no compunction about entering the haunted room alone. As she stood by the fireside a vapoury mist appeared, which gradually assumed the form of a red-haired, pale-faced boy, aged around 14. 'He had the solemn pallor of a tragedy beyond the endurance of a child,' Mrs Yeats later told her husband. She learnt that the ghostly boy was a member of the Blake family, the original owners of the house.

Shortly afterwards, with Gogarty away in England, his house fell victim to the Irish struggles and was burnt down by the IRA. 'Memories, nothing left now but memories ... and ten tall square towers, chimneys, stand bare on Europe's extreme verge,' lamented Gogarty. The house was rebuilt and Gogarty ran it as a hotel until relinquishing ownership in the 1950s.

Today the house is wonderfully atmospheric and ghosts still roam the corridors. In the past, guests have complained of sensing 'someone' in their room, and several ladies have had disturbing encounters with a man, whose reflection they have seen looking over their shoulders as they made up their faces in the mirror. Perhaps the last word on this mystery-steeped building should go to Oliver St John Gogarty. 'The countryside was magical,' he wrote, 'it is as if, in the faery land of Connemara at the extreme end of Europe, the incongruous flowed together at last, and the sweet and the bitter blended'

FANNY O'DEA'S
A pub that should not be passed

FANNY O'DEA'S ✗
LISSYCASEY, COUNTY CLARE
TEL: 0653 4143

During the winter assizes of 1790 Lord Norbury and his clerk were travelling from Kilrush to Ennis when they were caught in a fierce tempest. They sought shelter in a tiny roadside cottage, where the lady of the house made them most welcome. Soon a good fire was blazing in the hearth, their clothes drying before it. Enquiring if they would care to partake of a libation, the lady then produced two, piping hot, whiskey egg-flips. Lord Norbury was both amazed and delighted by this unexpected fare, and had enjoyed two more before he suddenly realized that, since his hostess did not possess a licence to sell intoxicating liquor he, as a judge, could in no way condone illicit trading by paying her for her hospitality. But by the same token he realized that 'life was precious and drinks were necessary' and so, there and then, he wrote out a licence entitling her to sell alcoholic beverages. And the name that licence bore was Fanny O'Dea.

In the years that followed Fanny O'Dea's fame spread far and wide and people travelled to Lissycasey just to partake of her legendary whiskey egg-flips. The business soon outgrew the little cottage, and more substantial premises were built on the other side of the road. The atmospheric old inn still thrives and has the distinction of being the oldest family-run pub in Ireland.

It is a spacious place, but has a dark and haunting ambience. In the central of its three bars a turf fire burns in a huge stone fireplace, its smoke wafting up a chimney that it has stained inky black. The fire has, reputedly, never been extinguished in over 150 years. The immense kitchen bar presents a bygone slice of rural Ireland, and has changed little since the 19th century. Old fiddles and farming implements hang from its dark beams. Behind the bar the draws, shelves and scales from the days when the premises doubled as a grocery store are still visible, as are antiquated tins of the provisions once sold. Fanny O'Dea's wedding ring is displayed in a glass case, and portraits of former owners and clients gaze down from the dark walls. Sadly, however, the whiskey egg-flips, for which the hostelry was once famous – made to a secret recipe handed down from Fanny O'Dea herself – are no longer served, and today's visitor must be content simply to read plaudits of this legendary tipple.

Although Fanny O'Dea's is not haunted in a conventional sense, there is an old tradition that it is unlucky to pass the pub without stopping in for a drink. This taboo had such a tight grip on the local imagination in days gone by that coachmen – and later omnibus drivers – would insist that their passengers pause for a libation to ward off ill fortune on the journey ahead.

Tradition holds that this superstition (or stroke of marketing genius!) arose in the early 19th century when a Kilrush man was sentenced to be hanged. As he was being transported to Ennis (where his execution was to be carried out) his guards asked if he would like to stop at Fanny O'Dea's for a final drink. The man declined; the cortège arrived in Ennis 30 minutes sooner than it should have, and he was hanged 30 minutes sooner than expected. Ten minutes later a horseman came galloping into town with the news that the man had been granted a pardon. Given that a stop at Fanny O'Dea's would have allowed the messenger enough time to deliver the reprieve and save the man's life, it soon became an established piece of local lore that ill luck awaited anyone who dared pass Fanny O'Dea's without stopping in for a drink.

MCCARTHY'S HOTEL
Publican, restaurant and undertaker!

The medieval town of Fethard has a wide High Street, lined by fine old shops, gracious Georgian houses and, as with many an Irish town, a decent selection of watering holes. Opposite its pretty church there stands a pub whose

McCarthy's Hotel ✖
Main Street
Fethard, County Tipperary
Tel: 0523 1149

reputation has spread far beyond the town's boundaries, and whose status borders almost on the legendary.

Richard McCarthy established McCarthy's Hotel in the 1840s, and supplied the local community with spirits, linen, groceries, bread, glass and china. He also provided hackney carriage services, accommodation and livery and, when his clients had reached the end of their allotted span, was called upon to bury them in his role as local undertaker. Although the business has been whittled down, it is still run by his descendents, and those who stray into the hotel's time-worn interior can still enjoy drinking and dining in the only place I know where the management advertises their business as 'Publican, Restaurant, Undertaker'!

The pub has hardly changed since the day Dick McCarthy opened for business. It has the lived-in look of a ragged old roué who has gambled and drunk his way to a raddled old age and is happy to have done so. It is the pub that time forgot, a deliciously eccentric establishment, the walls covered with yellowed newspapers and faded photographs. In some places paint peels from the walls; in others the walls peel from the paint! A curiously ornate wood-burning stove dominates the pub's forward section. Its flue meanders upwards before curving over and alarmingly close to the heads of customers seated at the bar. Andrew Lloyd Webber, whose castle is situated nearby, is a regular, and it was over a boozy session at McCarthy's that he and Ben Elton conceived the idea for their musical *The Beautiful Game*.

During the 1970s three formidable old ladies – Beatty, Kitty and Nell – successfully steered McCarthy's away from the trend for modernization that was afflicting Irish pubs. They stood out against change, and their lasting legacy is the timelessness with which McCarthy's is still imbued. The 21st century can do what it likes, for here the clock will always tick slowly.

McCarthy's most abiding supernatural occurrence is a harbinger of doom. Whenever a member of the family is about to die a picture falls off the wall for no apparent reason. This phenomenon occasionally accompanied by three loud knocks on the front door. Several other ghosts are known to frequent the atmospheric interior of the old pub, and customers have caught fleeting glimpses of wispy wraiths at all hours of the day and night. So if, as you sit in a dark corner supping your pint, you happen to spy someone sitting across from you, take a long hard look, and don't be surprised if they suddenly vanish!

KYTELER'S INN
The Kilkenny witch

Kyteler's Inn has a mysterious air. It is a lively, though atmospheric, venue with huge fireplaces, intriguing décor, and a cellar bar of dark stone arches and flagged floors that reminds one of a church crypt. It is the sort of place

KYTELER'S INN ✕
KIERAN STREET
KILKENNY, COUNTY KILKENNY
TEL: 056 21064

where, should the ghost choose to flit past you, your reaction would be simply to raise your glass in greeting and wish her a pleasant day!

Opposite: McCarthy's Bar in Fethard is a curious survivor of a bygone age. It is the only pub in Britain that advertises its services thus: 'Publican, Restaurant, Undertaker.'

Dame Alice Kyteler – from whom the inn derives its name – was born around the year 1280 and came from a Norman family. Her house stood on the site now occupied by Kyteler's Inn, and from here she conducted a thriving banking business, as well as possibly operating as an innkeeper. By 1324 she had married and been widowed three times. The fact that each union greatly increased her wealth led to a certain amount of jealousy among the good folk of Kilkenny, and by the time she came to plight her troth for a fourth time, to one John Le Poer, accusations of witchcraft were being levelled against her. Her enemies spread rumours that she had rid herself of her husbands by foul means, and that her wealth came courtesy of an evil spirit, whom she would conjure up in the guise of a great black dog. The numerous maidservants employed by her, it was rumoured, were fellow witches whose spells lured men into her evil clutches. Her chief accomplice in her demonic dabbling was said to be her lady-in waiting, Petronilla.

When word of Kilkenny's sinister sisterhood reached the local bishop, Richard de Ledrede, he determined to curb their activities. Unfortunately he had underestimated the power and influence of his adversary, and it was he who ended up imprisoned in Kilkenny Castle. However, Dame Alice's triumph was short-lived. The bishop secured his release and shortly thereafter, John d'Arcy, Ireland's Lord Justiciar, arrived in Kilkenny to arrest Dame Alice and Petronilla. Found guilty of witchcraft, they were sentenced to a public flogging, after which they were to be burnt at the stake.

But Dame Alice still had influential friends. On the night before her execution she escaped from prison and was smuggled to England, where her subsequent fate is unknown. Left to face the full wrath of the authorities alone, the unfortunate Petronilla made a full confession before being burnt to death before a vast multitude. It has long been rumoured that her ghost wanders the darker recesses of Kyteler's Inn, a shadowy figure that drifts slowly past astonished witnesses and which is described as being as benign a phantom as you could ever wish to chance upon.

THE CASTLE INN
The melancholic phantom

THE CASTLE INN ✗
5 LORD EDWARD STREET
DUBLIN
TEL: 01475 1122

Walls of solid stone, on which a diverse assortment of murderous-looking weaponry is displayed, gives this Dublin hostelry a castle-like feel. Michael Collins was a regular in the early 1900s. The poet James Clarence Mangan, whose works include the doleful ballad *Dark Rosaleen*, was born here on 1 May 1803, when it was a grocery and spirit store run by his cruel and oppressive father.

Mangan's adult life was blighted by depression, opium addiction and alcoholism. He died in the cholera epidemic that swept Dublin in 1849. His spirit is said to return to the place of his birth where his appearances are often presaged by a sudden drop in temperature and his passage marked by a feeling of melancholy.

JOHNNIE FOX'S PUB
Ireland's highest pub

The ancient road from Dublin city to Glencullen, via Rathfarnham – the 'High Road of Enniskerry' – twists and turns through the glorious scenery of the Dublin Mountains.

JOHNNIE FOX'S PUB ✕
GLENCULLEN, COUNTY DUBLIN
TEL: 01295 5647

A seemingly endless ascent will eventually bring you to Johnnie Fox's Pub, a true mountaintop lair which, at 1,000 feet (30 metres) above sea level, is the highest pub in Ireland.

It is a long, low building, with a cosy, welcoming dark porch. Its squat appearance belies a sprawling interior, where every available inch of wall space has been commandeered to display a rich array of memorabilia that would not seem out of place in some rural museum. Fading photographs, rakes, guns, farm tools, pennyfarthing bicycles – and even an 1840s coffin carrier, used to transport the deceased from the Mullingar workhouse to the mass graves situated nearby during the potato famine – are exhibited for the delectation of the curious tippler. Yet this is no 'theme' pub thrown up by some get-rich publican to make a quick Euro or two. This is a place that has, over the past 200 and more years, matured gracefully, and has now settled into a ripe old age.

Built in 1798, the year of the Irish uprising, Johnnie Fox's has several other associations with nationalist politics. Daniel O'Connell was a frequent visitor and held the first meeting of the Catholic Association within these walls. Later, Michael Collins set up an ammunitions factory in one of the inn's outbuildings.

More recently (and less controversially), Brad Pitt, Julia Roberts, Pierce Brosnan, The Rolling Stones, U2, Brian Keenan, John McCarthy and Salman Rushdie have set foot on the pub's flagstone floors, which are sprinkled with fresh sawdust each morning. ('That's not sawdust,' a barman once famously observed, 'that's last night's furniture!') Former US President Bill Clinton was meant to pay a visit, but his plans changed. His letter of apology is now framed on one of the walls.

The pub has had ample opportunity to acquire a resident ghost, although no one knows which of the former patrons graces the darker recesses of the older section. People sitting at tables here have often felt a light tap on their shoulders, but on turning around find that there is nobody behind them. Several visitors have enquired at the bar as to the identity of the old man in a brown jacket, whom they have seen sitting in the corner of the room and who appears to be gazing at nothing in particular.

'Oh don't worry about him,' reply the staff, 'he's just the ghost. He'll be leaving soon!'

KAVANAGH'S
The gravediggers' pub

KAVANAGH'S ✕
1 PROSPECT SQUARE
GLASNEVIN, COUNTY DUBLIN
TEL: 04046 6778

Founded in 1833 by John Kavanagh, a man who was blessed with 25 children, this quintessential Dublin boozer is still in the same family today, and its main bar remains plain and unembellished. It stands hard by Prospect (or Glasnevin) Cemetery, where lie the mortal remains of – among others – political emancipator Daniel O'Connell, 'the Liberator'; Britain's first female MP, Countess Markievicz (although because she was a member of Sinn Fein she didn't actually take her seat); Brendan Behan; Gerard Manley Hopkins; and nationalist leader Charles Stewart Parnell.

As a result of its proximity to the Dublin necropolis, most locals know the pub as 'The Gravediggers'. There was a time when the cemetery's railings came up very close to the Kavanagh's wall. Whenever the gravediggers fancied a pint they would tap the wall with their shovels or throw stones at it to attract the barman's attention. The walls still carry the scars of some of these 'requests!' No one is certain of the identity of the harmless ghost that sits at the bar, contentedly supping upon a phantom pint. He is said to be an elderly gentlemen, with a wispy grey beard and a butterfly collar on his shirt. Regulars and staff are happy to just let him be; if he wants to drink alone, that's fine!

Opposite: Johnnie Fox's is the highest pub in Ireland and, having reached its time-raddled walls, visitors can look forward to making the acquaintance of its brown-suited ghost.

THE BRAZEN HEAD
The patriot's ghost

THE BRAZEN HEAD ✕
20 LOWER BRIDGE STREET
DUBLIN
TEL:01679 5186

The Brazen Head is Dublin's oldest pub, though exactly how old is a matter of some debate. The sign outside states confidently that it dates from 1198, but this refers to an older hostelry on the site. The current establishment was built in 1750, and stands just a stone's throw away from the River Liffey.

You enter The Brazen Head's courtyard through a castellated gatehouse and step onto uneven cobblestones that deliver you to a lopsided doorway. Stumbling over the threshold, you find an atmospheric interior, cobwebbed with time, the air heavy with the smell of antiquity. An eclectic mix of customers huddle, almost conspiratorially around tables whose surfaces have matured to a rich darkness by years of spillage. Yellowing price lists and innumerable framed portraits vie for your attention against other pieces of memorabilia that hang on the dark and ancient walls. A large grandfather clock, which long ago gave up the struggle to display the correct time, keeps a stern watch on customers to the side of the older rear bar. And every so often the ghost of one of its more illustrious former patrons stumbles over the great divide and elicits cold shivers from those who chance upon him.

Robert Emmet was a leading figure in Ireland's battle for independence from English rule. He kept a room on the upper floor over The Brazen Head's main entrance, from which he could keep an eye on the comings and goings below, ever on the look-out for potential enemies. It was here that he planned the ill-fated 1803 Rising, which culminated in his capture and trial for high treason.

When asked if he had anything to say in response to his sentence, Emmet gave what is considered one of the most famous discourses of the period, his 'speech from the dock', in which he bravely expressed such noble and prophetic sentiments as, 'When my country takes her place among the nations of the earth, then shall my character be vindicated, then may my epitaph be written.'

Robert Emmet was hanged and beheaded on 20 September 1803. There is an ironic twist to the saga in that the man who executed him also frequented The Brazen Head, and the pub's clientele, aware of his notoriety, would often ask for their drink to be served in 'the hangman's glass'.

Robert Emmet's ghost is said to wander the premises at night, although he keeps more or less to himself. Witnesses only occasionally chance upon him as he drifts about the upper floors. From time to time, patrons become slightly agitated by the feeling that someone or something is watching them from one of the pub's dark corners. But any fear is momentary, and patrons who experience such impressions soon return to more important matters, such as enjoying the ambience of a pub that has long boasted it is open to all who arrive in a state 'in which they are fit to be received'.

FURTHER READING

Adams, Norman. *Haunted Scotland* (Mainstream, 1998)

Alexander, Marc. *Phantom Britain* (Muller, 1975)

Brooks, J.A. *Ghosts and Legends of the Lake District* (Jarrold, 1988)

Brooks, J.A. *Ghosts and Witches of the Cotswolds* (Jarrold, 1981)

Byrne, Thomas. *Tales From The Past* (Ironmarket, 1977)

Clarke, David. *Ghosts and Legends of the Peak District* (Jarrold, 1991)

Coventry, Martin. *Haunted Places of Scotland* (Goblinshead, 1999)

Coxe, Anthony D. Hippisley. *Haunted Britain* (Pan, 1975)

Curran, Bob. *Banshees, Beasts and Brides from the Sea* (Appletree Press, 1996)

Dunne, John J. *Irish Ghosts* (Appletree Press, 1977)

Folklore, Myths and Legends of Britain (Readers Digest Association Limited, 1977)

Green, Andrew. *Our Haunted Kingdom* (Fontana/Collins, 1973)

Hallam, Jack. *The Haunted Inns of England* (Wolfe, 1972)

Harper, Charles. *Haunted Houses* (Bracken, reprint 1993)

Jeffery, P.H. *Ghosts, Legends and Lore of Wales* (Orchard)

Jones, Richard. *Haunted Britain and Ireland* (New Holland, 2001)

Jones, Richard. *Haunted Castles of Britain and Ireland* (New Holland, 2003)

Jones, Richard. *Myths and Legends of Britain and Ireland* (New Holland, 2003)

Jones, Richard. *Walking Dickensian London* (New Holland, 2003)

Jones, Richard. *Walking Haunted London* (New Holland, 1999)

Long, Roger. *Reputedly Haunted Inns of the Chilterns and Thames Valley* (Woodfield, 1993)

Love, Dane. *The Auld Inns of Scotland* (Robert Hale, 1997)

Maddox, Brenda. *George's Ghosts: A New Life of W.B. Yeats* (Picador, 1999)

Marsden, Simon. *The Haunted Realm* (Little, Brown 1986)

Mason, John. *Haunted Heritage* (Collins and Brown, 1999)

Pipe, Marian and Butler, Mia. *Walks in Mysterious Northamptonshire* (Sigma Leisure, 1999)

Playfair, Guy Lion. *The Haunted Pub Guide* (Javelin, 1987)

Puttick, Betty. *Ghosts of Essex* (Countryside, 1997)

Puttick, Betty. *Ghosts of Hertfordshire* (Countryside, 1994)

Seafield, Lily. *Scottish Ghosts* (Lomond, 1999)

Timpson, John. *Timpson's English Country Inns* (Headline, 1995)

Turner, Mark. *Folklore and Mysteries of the Cotswolds* (Hale, 1993)

Underwood, Peter. *This Haunted Isle* (Javelin, 1986)

INDEX

ACKNOWLEDGEMENTS

Many people have helped with the research and writing of this book. Staff at local libraries were ever willing to dig out old newspaper cuttings or books that provided me with details on haunted pubs in their region. I am also indebted to the staff at innumerable Tourist Information Centres for their invaluable input. Managers and customers at many pubs proved to be goldmines of information, either by alerting me to new hauntings on their premises or directing me to other haunted hostelries in their locale. Pete Farmer, Lindsay Siviter, Karen Arcay and Lez Ellis were just a few of the other people who helped my researches. The people at the Fat Badgers website proved invaluable for their advice on inns and taverns worth visiting.

To every one of you (and those I haven't mentioned), I proffer my sincere thanks and, as promised, have raised a glass (or two) to celebrate the end of the journey!

At New Holland Publishers I'd like to thank Jo Hemmings for her support, Deborah Taylor for her patience and Gülen Shevki for her design work. I'd also like to thank Chris Coe for his photography.

On a personal level I'd like to thank my sister, Geraldine Hennigan, for listening and offering advice. My wife, Joanne, for enduring (or perhaps even celebrating) my long absences, and my sons, Thomas and William, for making my returns so memorable.

Finally, to those whose stories, be they tragic or otherwise, have made this book possible, long may you wander – but may you always be at peace.